Houghton Mifflin
Reading

Teacher's Edition

Kindergarten

Friends Together

Senior Authors J. David Cooper, John J. Pikulski

Authors David J. Chard, Gilbert G. Garcia, Claude N. Goldenberg, Phyllis C. Hunter, Marjorie Y. Lipson, Shane Templeton, Sheila W. Valencia, MaryEllen Vogt

Consultants Linda H. Butler, Linnea C. Ehri, Carla B. Ford

HOUGHTON MIFFLIN   BOSTON

LITERATURE REVIEWERS

Consultants: Dr. Adela Artola Allen, Associate Dean, Graduate College, Associate Vice President for Inter-American Relations, University of Arizona, Tucson, AZ; **Dr. Manley Begay,** Co-director of the Harvard Project on American Indian Economic Development, Director of the National Executive Education Program for Native Americans, Harvard University, John F. Kennedy School of Government, Cambridge, MA; **Dr. Nicholas Kannellos,** Director, Arte Publico Press, Director, Recovering the U.S. Hispanic Literacy Heritage Project, University of Houston, TX; **Mildred Lee,** author and former head of Library Services for Sonoma County, Santa Rosa, CA; **Dr. Barbara Moy,** Director of the Office of Communication Arts, Detroit Public Schools, MI; **Norma Naranjo,** Clark County School District, Las Vegas, NV; **Dr. Arlette Ingram Willis,** Associate Professor, Department of Curriculum and Instruction, Division of Language and Literacy, University of Illinois at Urbana-Champaign, IL

Teachers: Helen Brooks, Vestavia Hills Elementary School, Birmingham, Alabama; **Patricia Buchanan,** Thurgood Marshall School, Newark, Delaware; **Gail Connor,** Language Arts Resource Teacher, Duval County, Jacksonville, Florida; **Vicki DeMott,** McLean Science/Technology School, Wichita, Kansas; **Marge Egenhoffer,** Dixon Elementary School, Brookline, Wisconsin; **Mary Jew Mori,** Griffin Avenue Elementary, Los Angeles, California

PROGRAM REVIEWERS

Linda Bayer, Jonesboro, GA; **Sheri Blair,** Warner Robins, GA; **Faye Blake,** Jacksonville, FL; **Suzi Boyett,** Sarasota, FL; **Carol Brockhouse,** Madison Schools, Wayne Westland Schools, MI; **Patti Brustad,** Sarasota, FL; **Jan Buckelew,** Venice, FL; **Maureen Carlton,** Barstow, CA; **Karen Cedar,** Gold River, CA; **Karen Ciraulo,** Folsom, CA; **Marcia M. Clark,** Griffin, GA; **Kim S. Coady,** Covington, GA; **Eva Jean Conway,** Valley View School District, IL; **Marilyn Crownover,** Tustin, CA; **Carol Daley,** Sioux Falls, SD; **Jennifer Davison,** West Palm Beach, FL; **Lynne M. DiNardo,** Covington, GA; **Kathy Dover,** Lake City, GA; **Cheryl Dultz,** Citrus Heights, CA; **Debbie Friedman,** Fort Lauderdale, FL; **Anne Gaitor,** Lakeland, GA; **Rebecca S. Gillette,** Saint Marys, GA; **Buffy C. Gray,** Peachtree City, GA; **Merry Guest,** Homestead, FL; **Jo Nan Holbrook,** Lakeland, GA; **Beth Holguin,** San Jose, CA; **Coleen Howard-Whals,** St. Petersburg, FL; **Beverly Hurst,** Jacksonville, FL; **Debra Jackson,** St. Petersburg, FL; **Vickie Jordan,** Centerville, GA; **Cheryl Kellogg,** Panama City, FL; **Karen Landers,** Talladega County, AL; **Barb LeFerrier,** Port Orchard, WA; **Sandi Maness,** Modesto, CA; **Ileana Masud,** Miami, FL; **David Miller,** Cooper City, FL; **Muriel Miller,** Simi Valley, CA; **Walsetta W. Miller,** Macon, GA; **Jean Nielson,** Simi Valley, CA; **Sue Patton,** Brea, CA; **Debbie Peale,** Miami, FL; **Loretta Piggee,** Gary, IN; **Jennifer Rader,** Huntington, CA; **April Raiford,** Columbus, GA; **Cheryl Remash,** Manchester, NH; **Francis Rivera,** Orlando, FL; **Marina Rodriguez,** Hialeah, FL; **Marilynn Rose,** MI; **Kathy Scholtz,** Amesbury, MA; **Kimberly Moulton Schorr,** Columbus, GA; **Linda Schrum,** Orlando, FL; **Sharon Searcy,** Mandarin, FL; **Melba Sims,** Orlando, FL; **Judy Smith,** Titusville, FL; **Bea Tamo,** Huntington, CA; **Dottie Thompson,** Jefferson County, AL; **Dana Vassar,** Winston-Salem, NC; **Beverly Wakefield,** Tarpon Springs, FL; **Joy Walls,** Winston-Salem, NC; **Elaine Warwick,** Williamson County, TN; **Audrey N. Watkins,** Atlanta, GA; **Marti Watson,** Sarasota, FL

Supervisors: Judy Artz, Butler County, OH; **James Bennett,** Elkhart, IN; **Kay Buckner-Seal,** Wayne County, MI; **Charlotte Carr,** Seattle, WA; **Sister Marion Christi,** Archdiocese of Philadelphia, PA; **Alvina Crouse,** Denver, CO; **Peggy DeLapp,** Minneapolis, MN; **Carol Erlandson,** Wayne Township Schools, IN; **Brenda Feeney,** North Kansas City School District, MO; **Winnie Huebsch,** Sheboygan, WI; **Brenda Mickey,** Winston-Salem, NC; **Audrey Miller,** Camden, NJ; **JoAnne Piccolo,** Westminster, CO; **Sarah Rentz,** Baton Rouge, LA; **Kathy Sullivan,** Omaha, NE; **Rosie Washington,** Gary, IN; **Theresa Wishart,** Knox County Public Schools, TN

English Language Learners Reviewers: Maria Arevalos, Pomona, CA; **Lucy Blood,** NV; **Manuel Brenes,** Kalamazoo, MI; **Delight Diehn,** AZ; **Susan Dunlap,** Richmond, CA; **Tim Fornier,** Grand Rapids, MI; **Connie Jimenez,** Los Angeles, CA; **Diane Bonilla Lether,** Pasadena, CA; **Anna Lugo,** Chicago, IL; **Marcos Martel,** Hayward, CA; **Carolyn Mason,** Yakima, WA; **Jackie Pinson,** Moorpark, CA; **Jenaro Rivas,** NJ; **Jerilyn Smith,** Salinas, CA; **Noemi Velazquez,** Jersey City, NJ; **JoAnna Veloz,** NJ; **Dr. Santiago Veve,** Las Vegas, NV

Printed in China

ISBN-13: 978-0-61862-835-3
ISBN-10: 0-61862-835-5

3 4 5 6 7 8 9 10 L 12 11 10 09 08 07

CREDITS

Cover
Cover Illustration by Dave Clegg.

Photography
Theme Opener © IT International Ltd./eStock Photo.

Assignment Photography
T25 © HMCo./Dorey Sparre.
All other photography © HMCo./Joel Benjamin.

Illustration
T85 Dennis Hockerman. **T143** Pierre Pratt.
Theme Class Project art by Tim Johnson.
All other child art by Morgan-Cain & Associates.

ACKNOWLEDGMENTS

Grateful acknowledgment is made for permission to reprint copyrighted material as follows:

Theme 4
Aaron and Gayla's Alphabet Book, by Eloise Greenfield. Illustrations by Jan Spivy Gilchrist. Text copyright © 1993 by Eloise Greenfield. Illustrations copyright © 1993 by Jan Spivey Gilchrist. Reprinted by arrangement with Black Butterfly Children's Books/Writers and Readers Publishing, Inc.

Friends Together

OBJECTIVES

Phonemic Awareness blending and segmenting onset and rime; blending phonemes ·

Phonics sounds *H, h; V, v; C, c;* words with short *a*

High-Frequency Words *a, to*

Reading Strategies question; phonics/decoding; predict/infer; evaluate

Comprehension Skills text organization and summarizing; cause and effect

Vocabulary position words; action words

Fluency build reading fluency

Concepts of Print word spacing; first letter; spoken words to print

Writing newsletter; story; note; list

Listening/Speaking/Viewing supports vocabulary and writing

Friends Together

CONTENTS

Week 1

Big Book

Skill Lessons. See Daily Lesson Plans.

Books for Small-Group Reading

Nonfiction

Decodable
Text

On My Way
Practice Reader
Below Level/On Level
(Week 3)

Leveled Reader
On Level

Little Big Book
On Level/Above Level

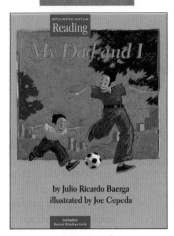
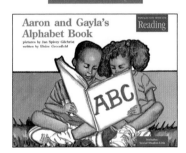

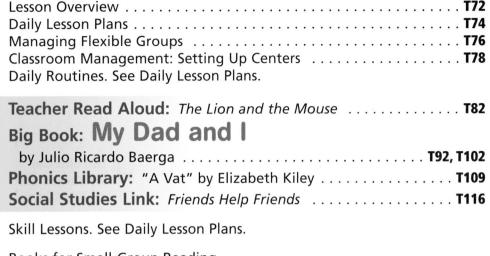

Bibliography

BOOKS FOR SMALL-GROUP READING, READ ALOUD, AND FLUENCY BUILDING

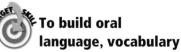 **To build oral language, vocabulary and fluency**, choose books from this list for additional read aloud opportunities and small-group reading.

Key

 Science

 Social Studies

 Multicultural

 Music

 Math

 Classic

 Art

 Career

Classroom Bookshelf

BOOKS FOR BROWSING

Biscuit's Big Friend
by Alyssa Satin Capucilli
Harper 2003 (32p)
Biscuit the puppy has trouble keeping up with his new friend, a big dog named Sam.

My Friend Rabbit
by Eric Rohmann
Roaring Brook 2002 (32p)
Rabbit's attempts to help his friend Mouse lead to trouble in this Caldecott Medal story.

 Where Are You Going? To See My Friend!
by Eric Carle and Kazuo Iwamura
Orchard 2003 (32p)
*A dog, off to meet a friend, invites other animals to come along. **Text in English and Japanese**.*

Gossie and Gertie
by Olivier Dunrea
Houghton 2002 (32p)
Goslings Gossie and Gertie, best friends, do almost everything together.

Hi, Harry!
by Martin Waddell
Candlewick 2003 (32p)
Harry the tortoise tries to find a friend who'll play with him at his own slow speed.

Four Friends Together
by Sue Heap
Candlewick 2003 (32p)
A girl and her animal friends enjoy a story together.

 Two Girls Can
by Keiko Narahashi
McElderry 2000 (32p)
Two girls celebrate all the things that friends can do together.

 Dear Daisy, Get Well Soon
by Maggie Smith
Crown 2000 (32p) also paper
When Daisy gets the chicken pox, Peter proves he's a friend she can count on.

 Best Friends
by Marcia Leonard
Millbrook 1999 (32p) also paper
Two girls are best friends even though they're different in many ways.

BOOKS FOR TEACHER READ ALOUD

Chicken Chickens Go to School
by Valeri Gorbachev
North-South 2003 (32p)
Two shy chickens worry that they won't make friends on their first day of school.

 Simon and Molly Plus Hester
by Lisa Jahn-Clough
Houghton 2001 (32p)
When Hester moves into the neighborhood, Simon fears he'll lose Molly as his best friend.

That's What Friends Are For
by F. Parry Heide and S. Van Clief
Candlewick 2003 (32p)
Elephant's friends are good at giving advice, but only Opposum solves his problem.

 One for Me, One for You
by C. C. Cameron
Roaring Brook 2003 (32p)
Two friends find a perfect solution to sharing three cookies.

 Ira Sleeps Over*
by Bernard Waber
Houghton 1972 (48p) also paper
Spending the night at his friend Reggie's, Ira worries about not having his teddy bear.

 My Steps
by Sally Derby
Lee & Low 1996 (32p) also paper
*An African American girl and her friends have fun playing on the front steps of her city home. **Available in Spanish as** Mi escalera.*

 Best Friends for Frances
by Russell Hoban
Harper 1969 (32p) also paper
Frances the badger teaches her next-door neighbor Albert about friendship.

The Best of Friends
by Pirkko Vainio
North-South 2000 (32p)
Hare likes carrots and Bear prefers fish, but despite their differences, the two are good friends.

 My Friend and I*
by Lisa Jahn-Clough
Houghton 1999 (32p)
A boy and girl discover sharing is more fun then fighting.

*Included in Classroom Bookshelf, Level K

Friends!
by Elaine Scott
Simon 2000 (32p)
Photographs and text introduce friends and the activities they share.

 A Letter to Amy
by Ezra Jack Keats
Harper 1968 (32p) also paper

Peter rushes out in a thunderstorm to send his friend Amy an invitation to his party.

Friend Frog
by Alma Flor Ada
Harcourt 2000 (32p)
Field Mouse can't jump or swim like the frog he meets at the pond, but they become friends.

A Summery Saturday Morning
by Margaret Mahy
Viking 1998 (32p)
A group of friends and their dogs enjoy a lively walk on a summer morning.

 May I Bring a Friend?
by Beatrice Schenk de Regniers
Macmillan 1964 (32p) also paper

A boy invited to tea with the king and queen takes along his animal friends in this repetitive, rhyming story.

 Bein' With You This Way
by W. Nikola-Lisa
Lee & Low 1995 (32p) also paper
In cumulative rhyme, a girl rounds up a group of friends for fun in the park. **Available in Spanish as** La alegría de ser tú y yo.

BOOKS FOR PHONICS READ ALOUD

Scat, Cats!
by Joan Holub
Viking 2001 (32p)
A boy and girl shoo some troublesome cats out of their house, but miss them when they're gone.

That Is Not My Hat!
by Cecilia Venn
Millbrook 1999 (48p)

Kate and her friends help her brother Sam find his lost hat.

The Visitor
by Patrice Aggs
Orchard 1999 (32p)
Kittens Cosy and Posy discover that someone very different from themselves can be a good friend.

Technology

Computer Software Resources

- **Lexia Quick Phonics Assessment CD-ROM**
- **Lexia Phonics Intervention CD-ROM: Primary**
- **Published by Sunburst Technology***
  Tenth Planet™ Vowels: Short and Long
  Curious George® Pre-K ABCs
  First Phonics
- **Published by The Learning Company**
  Dr. Seuss's ABC™
  Paint, Write, & Play!™
  ¡Vamos a Jugar, Pintar, y Escribir!
- **Animals Alike CD-ROM.** *Heinemann*

Video Cassettes

- **A Weekend with Wendell** *by Kevin Henkes. Weston Woods*
- **Corduroy** *by Don Freeman. Weston Woods*
- **Happy Birthday, Moon** *by Frank Asch. Weston Woods*
- **Frog and Toad Are Friends** *by Arnold Lobel. Weston Woods*
- **Frog and Toad Together** *by Arnold Lobel. Weston Woods*

Audio

- **Jamaica Tag-Along** *by Juanita Havill. Houghton*
- **Ira Sleeps Over** *by Bernard Waber. Houghton*
- **Bein' With You This Way** *by W. Nikola-Lisa. Live Oak*
- **Mitchell Is Moving** *by Marjorie Weinman Sharmat. Live Oak*
- **May I Bring a Friend?** *by Beatrice Schenk de Regniers. Weston Woods*
- **CD-ROM for** *Friends Together* *Houghton Mifflin Company*

* ©Sunburst Technology. All Rights Reserved.
Technology Resources addresses are on page R14.

Education Place

www.eduplace.com *Log on to Education Place for more activities relating to* Friends Together.

Book Adventure

www.bookadventure.org *This Internet reading-incentive program provides thousands of titles for children to read.*

*Included in Classroom Bookshelf, Level K

Theme Skills Overview

	Week 1

Pacing
Approximately 3 weeks

Teacher Read Aloud
Friends at School
Fiction

Big Book
Aaron and Gayla's Alphabet Book
Fiction

See the **Combination Classroom Planning Guide** for lesson planning and management support.

Combination Classrooms

Learning to Read
Phonemic Awareness

Phonics

Concepts of Print

High-Frequency Words

Comprehension

- **Blending and Segmenting Onset and Rime** T
- **Blending Phonemes** T
- **Beginning Sound /h/**
- **Initial Consonant** *h* T
- **Blending Short** *a* **Words** T
- **Concepts of Print** T
- **High-Frequency Word:** *a* T

Guiding Comprehension

- **Text Organization and Summarizing** T
- **Comprehension Strategy: Question**
- **Decodable Text**

"Nat at Bat"

Social Studies Link *We Read Together*
Nonfiction

Vocabulary Readers

Nonfiction

Books for Small-Group Reading
- Fluency Practice
- Independent Reading

- **Word and Picture Book**
- **Take-Home Phonics Library**
- **Vocabulary Reader**
- **Leveled Reader**
- **Little Big Book**

Leveled Readers

Word Work
High-Frequency Word Practice

Building Words

High-Frequency Words: *I, see, my, like, a*
- **Words with Short** *a*

✹ Half-Day Kindergarten

Focus on lessons for tested skills marked with **T**.
Then choose other activities as time allows.

Writing and Oral Language
Vocabulary

Writing

Listening/Speaking/Viewing

- **Vocabulary Reader**
- **Vocabulary: Using Position Words**
- ✏ **Shared Writing:** Writing a Newsletter
- **Interactive Writing:** Using Position Words
- **Independent Writing:** Recording Information
- Listening/Speaking/Viewing

T Skill tested on Emerging Literacy Survey, Integrated Theme Test and/or Weekly or Theme Skills Test

Target Skills

Phonemic Awareness	
Phonics	
Comprehension	
Vocabulary	
Fluency	

Cross-Curricular Activities

Week 1:
Setting Up Centers Activities
Theme Class Project

Week 2:
Setting Up Centers Activities
Theme Class Project

Week 3:
Setting Up Centers Activities
Theme Class Project

Week 2

Teacher Read Aloud
The Lion and the Mouse
Fiction

Big Book
My Dad and I
Fiction

- **Blending and Segmenting Onset and Rime** T
- **Blending Phonemes** T
- **Beginning Sound /v/**
- **Initial Consonant v** T
- **Blending Short a Words** T
- **Concepts of Print,** T
- **High-Frequency Word: to** T

Guiding Comprehension

- **Cause and Effect** T
- **Comprehension Strategy: Predict/Infer**
- **Decodable Text**

"A Vat"

Social Studies Link *Friends Help Friends*
Nonfiction

- **Word and Picture Book**
- **Take-Home Phonics Library**
- **Vocabulary Reader**
- **Leveled Reader**
- **Little Big Book**

High-Frequency Words: *a, I, like, my, see, to*

- **Words with Short a**

Vocabulary Reader

- **Vocabulary: Using Action Words**

- **Shared Writing:** Writing a Story
- **Interactive Writing:** Writing Sentences
- **Independent Writing:** Journals
- Listening/Speaking/Viewing

Week 3: Tested Skill Review

Teacher Read Aloud
Stone Soup
Fiction

Big Books
Aaron and Gayla's Alphabet Book
My Dad and I

- **Blending and Segmenting Onset and Rime** T
- **Blending Phonemes** T
- **Beginning Sound /k/**
- **Initial Consonant c; Blending Short a Words** T
- **Concepts of Print,** T
- **High-Frequency Words: a, to** T

Guiding Comprehension

- **Cause and Effect** T
- **Text Organization and Summarizing** T
- **Comprehension Strategy: Question/Evaluate**
- **Decodable Text**

"Cat Sat"

Revisit the Links *We Read Together* and *Friends Help Friends*

- **On My Way Practice Reader**
- **Word and Picture Book**
- **Take-Home Phonics Library**
- **Vocabulary Reader**
- **Leveled Reader**   **Little Big Book**

High-Frequency Words: *a, I, like, my, see, to*

- **Words with Short a**

Vocabulary Reader

- **Vocabulary: Using Action Words**

- **Shared Writing:** Writing a Note
- **Interactive Writing:** Writing a List
- **Independent Writing:** Journals
- Listening/Speaking/Viewing

Concepts of Print lessons teach important foundational skills for Phonics.

Additional Books for Small-Group Reading

Little Readers for Guided Reading
Use these books to check children's fluency progress.

Additional Theme Resources

- Challenge/Extension Activities
- Blackline Masters
- Songs
- Word Lists

Technology

Education Place
www.eduplace.com

Log on to Education Place for more activities relating to *Friends Together*.

Lesson Planner CD-ROM
Customize your planning for *Friends Together* with the Lesson Planner CD-ROM.

Curious George® Learns Phonics
Contains interactive phonics activities for beginning readers.

Management Routines

Quiet Time

When children are restless and you want them to calm down for story or quiet time, use a Mousekin puppet and the rhyme that follows.

To make the puppet, follow these steps:

- Cut the thumb off an old pair of gloves.
- Draw Mousekin on the thumb.
- Add a pink nose, a tiny mouth, some whiskers, and two pointed ears.

Sit in the circle with your gloved thumb hidden inside your hand. Recite this poem in a small, small voice. Children will soon quiet and wait for Mousekin to POP out of his house.

Quiet Time

Tiny little thumbkin Mouse

Lives inside his tiny house.

When you're quiet as can be,

A little Mousekin you will see.

A Little Whisper

Your voice is a powerful tool in classroom management. The more quietly you speak, the more quiet children often become. Try whispering to a noisy group of kindergartners. They soon begin to whisper themselves.

Instructional Routines

Blending Routines Cards

In this theme children begin using their knowledge of phonics to help them read whole words. While the procedures for modeling the blending routine are described in the phonics lessons, you may want to have a summary of the steps to refer to at group time or to share with other adults who work with your students. Use the **Blending Routines Cards** as a handy reference tool.

The first card, *Continuous Blending,* outlines the steps used in the phonics lessons in Themes 4–10. For children who have difficulty mastering the routine after several attempts or who need help with longer words, try the variations called *Sound-by-Sound Blending* or *Vowel-First Blending,* which provide other approaches to remembering and blending sounds sequentially.

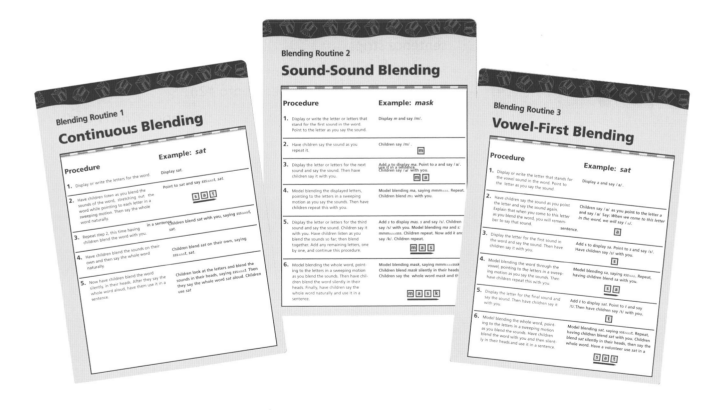

Theme Class Project

Independent Activities

Have children work on this theme project at any time during the theme while you work with small groups.

Additional Independent Activities

- **Classroom Management Handbook,** pp. 74–97

- **Challenge Handbook,** pp. 24–31

- Setting Up Centers, pp.T22–T23, T78–T79, T136–T137

Look for more activities in the Classroom Management Kit.

The Friendly Book

Materials sentence strips • drawing paper • crayons or markers • glue • string • stapler ·········

Making Theme Connections

Before beginning the project, display theme resources such as the **Theme Poster,** the Theme Poem, and **Big Books**. Initiate a discussion about the concepts of friendship and what friends do for each other.

What to Do

- Have each child choose another child and tell what they like doing together. If children seem to be hesitant about sharing in a group, see if having a puppet "do the talking" will help.

- Record children's responses on sentence strips. (See Photo #1.)

- When all children have been included, distribute the completed sentence strips.

- Have each child glue a sentence strip onto drawing paper and illustrate the response. (See Photo #2.)

- Assemble the pages to make a big class book, *The Friendly Book*. Bind the class book together with staples or string. (See Photo #3.)

- Together read the book. During the theme, display *The Friendly Book* in the Book Center for children to share and read together. (See Photo #4.)

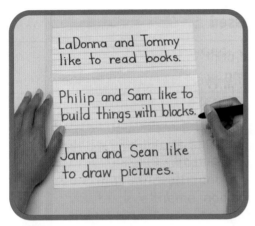

1 Record children's responses on sentence strips.

2 Have children illustrate their responses.

3 Assemble the pages to make a class book, *The Friendly Book*.

4 Display the book in the Book Center.

REACHING ALL LEARNERS

Challenge

Discuss how children all over the world have friends. There's a word for friend in most languages. Teach children the word in Spanish (*amigo*); French (*ami*); German (*freund*); Italian (*amico*); Swahili (*rafiki*). Some children may want to label pictures with one of these words.

Planning for Assessment

During instruction in Theme 4 . . .

1 SCREENING AND DIAGNOSIS

If you have used the **Emerging Literacy Survey** to determine children's levels in phonemic awareness, letter recognition, and beginning decoding skills, you might want to readminister all or parts of the survey for continuing diagnosis.

Section	Areas Assessed
Familiarity with Print	• Concepts of print • Letter naming
Phonemic Awareness	• Rhyme • Beginning sounds • Blending and segmenting onsets and rimes • Blending and segmenting phonemes
Beginning Reading and Writing	• Word recognition • Word writing • Sentence dictation

To determine individual children's specific instructional needs and to plan instruction, you might consider readministering one or both of the following tests:

- **Leveled Reading Passages Assessment Kit**
- **Lexia Quick Phonics Assessment CD-ROM**

2 MONITORING PROGRESS

To ensure that children are making adequate progress throughout the theme, use the following resources:

- Monitoring Student Progress boxes
- Theme 4 Observation Checklist
- Themes 1–4 **Integrated Theme Test**
- Theme 4 **Weekly Skills Tests** or **Theme Skills Tests**
- **Emerging Literacy Survey** (See above.)

3 MANAGING AND REPORTING

Technology To manage your assessment information, record each child's performance on the **Learner Profile CD-ROM**.

Kindergarten Benchmarks
Documenting Adequate Yearly Progress

For your planning, listed here are the instructional goals and activities that help develop benchmark behaviors for kindergartners. Use this list to plan instruction and to monitor children's progress. See the checklist of skills found on TE page T185.

Theme Lessons and Activities

Benchmark Behaviors

Listening Comprehension/Oral Language/Vocabulary

- songs, rhymes, chants, finger plays
- story discussions

- listen to a story attentively
- participate in story discussions

Phonemic Awareness

- blending and segmenting onset and rime
- blending phonemes

- blend sounds into meaningful units

Phonics

- initial consonants *h, c, v*
- short *a* words

- name single letters and their sounds
- decode some common CVC words

Concepts of Print

- word spacing
- matching speech to print

- recognize common print conventions

Reading and Fluency

- decodable texts

- read and write a few words

Vocabulary: High-Frequency Words

- high-frequency words *a, to*

- select a letter to represent a sound

Comprehension

- text organization and summarizing
- cause and effect

- think critically about a text
- use effective reading strategies

Writing and Language

- writing simple phrases or sentences
- using action words

- label pictures using phonetic spellings
- write independently

Launching the Theme

Theme 4: Friends Together
Copyright © Houghton Mifflin Company. All rights reserved.
1-43570-K Photography by (t) DWA/Dann Tardif/The Stock Market; (tr) Peter Correz/Tony Stone Images; (m) Rubberball Productions; (bl) Lori Adamski Peek/Tony Stone Images; (br) Arthur Tilley/Tony Stone Images

Using the Theme Poster

Display the Theme Poster and discuss the photograph. Ask, How is a Crossing Guard your friend? How is a pet a friend? Is your big brother or sister your friend, too? If you could add a photograph to this poster, whose picture would you add?

Use the Theme Poster throughout the theme. Tack up the poster in a prominent spot and add photographs, drawings, and collages as extensions to the ideas listed.

- **Week 1:** After reading *Friends at School,* have children talk about new Kindergarten friends. Take pictures, if possible, of children with their friends. Add pictures to the **Theme Poster** display.

- **Week 2:** Children draw people in their families who are also friends. Tell children they can include extended family members as well as parents.

- **Week 3:** Discuss community helpers as children read the **Social Studies Link** *Friends Help Friends.* Add drawings of school or community helpers to the poster display.

Theme Poem: "My Teddy Bear"

Have children describe what they see in the illustration.

- Stretch them to use descriptive language such as *tan, soft, cuddly, furry.*
- Read the poem aloud.
- Ask, What do you think the poet meant by saying a teddy bear is a *faithful* friend?

Read aloud other poems. Poems help develop children's oral comprehension and listening skills. You may want to choose other poems to read aloud from *Higglety Pigglety: A Book of Rhymes*.

My Teddy Bear

A teddy bear is a faithful friend.
You can pick him up at either end.
His fur is the color of breakfast toast,
And he's always there when you need him most.

18

Higglety Pigglety: A Book of Rhymes, **page 18**

Monitoring Student Progress

Monitoring Progress

Throughout the theme, monitor your children's progress by using the following program features in the **Teacher's Edition:**

- Guiding Comprehension questions
- Literature response groups
- Skill lesson applications
- Monitoring Student Progress boxes
- Theme Wrap-Up, pages T184–T185

Classroom Management

At any time during the theme, you can assign the Theme Class Project on **Teacher Edition** pages T10–T11 while you provide differentiated instruction to small groups.

Additional independent activity centers related to specific selections can be found in the **Teacher's Edition.**

- Setting Up Centers, Week 1, pages T22–T23
- Setting Up Centers, Week 2, pages T78–T79
- Setting Up Centers, Week 3, pages T136–T137

Home Connection

Send home the theme newsletter for *Friends Together* to introduce the theme and suggest home activities (See **Teacher's Resource Blackline Masters 59–60.**)

For other suggestions relating to *Friends Together,* see **Home/ Community Connections.**

Lesson Overview

Literature

Aaron and Gayla's Alphabet Book

pictures by Jan Spivey Gilchrist
written by Eloise Greenfield

HOUGHTON MIFFLIN
Reading

Includes:
Social Studies Link

⭐ **Selection Summary**

Two friends share lots of fun—all the way from A to Z.

1 Teacher Read Aloud

• *Friends at School*

2 Big Book

• *Aaron and Gayla's Alphabet Book*
Genre: Realistic Fiction

3 Decodable Text

Phonics Library

• "Nat at Bat"

4 Social Studies Link

This Link appears after the main Big Book selection.

Leveled Books

Vocabulary Reader

- Below Level, ELL
- Lesson
- Take-Home Version

Leveled Reader

- On Level, Above Level
- Lesson
- Take-Home Version

Instructional Support

Planning and Practice

Planning and Classroom Management

Reading and skill instruction

Plans and activities for reaching all learners

- Newsletters
- Observation Checklists
- Theme Activity Masters

- Phonemic Awareness
- Letter Recognition
- Phonics Practice

Independent practice for skills

Fluency Practice: Word and Picture Books

- Phonics Practice
- Word Building

Reaching All Learners

Coordinated lessons, activities, and projects for additional reading instruction for

- Classroom Teacher
- Extended Day
- Pull Out
- Resource Teacher

Technology

 Audio Selection
Aaron and Gayla's Alphabet Book

www.eduplace.com

Daily Lesson Plans

Technology
Lesson Planner CD-ROM allows you to customize the chart below to develop your own lesson plans.

T Skill tested on Weekly or Theme Skills Test and/or Integrated Theme Test

WEEK 1 **DAILY LESSON PLANS**

⏱ 60–90 minutes

Learning to Read

Phonemic Awareness

Phonics

High-Frequency Words

Comprehension

Concepts of Print

Vocabulary Reader
Where Is the Dog?

Leveled Reader
We Like To Play!

⏱ 30–45 minutes

Word Work

High-Frequency Word Practice

Building Words

⏱ 30–45 minutes

Writing and Oral Language

Vocabulary

Writing

Listening/Speaking/Viewing

DAY 1

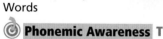
FRIENDS AT SCHOOL

Daily Routines, *T24–T25*
Calendar, Message, High-Frequency Words

⊙ **Phonemic Awareness** T

Teacher Read Aloud, *T26–T27*

⊙ **Comprehension Strategy,** *T26*
Question

⊙ **Comprehension Skill,** *T26*
Text Organization and Summarizing T

⊙ **Phonemic Awareness,** *T28–T29*
Beginning Sound /h/ T

Leveled Reader

High-Frequency Word Practice, *T30*
Words: *I, my, like*

⊙ **Oral Language: Vocabulary,** *T31*
Using Position Words

Vocabulary Reader

DAY 2

Aaron and Gayla's Alphabet Book

Daily Routines, *T32–T33*
Calendar, Message, High-Frequency Words

⊙ **Phonemic Awareness** T

Reading the Big Book, *T34–T35*

⊙ **Comprehension Strategy,** *T34*
Question

⊙ **Comprehension Skill,** *T34*
Text Organization and Summarizing T

⊙ **Phonics,** *T36–T37*
Initial Consonant *h* T

⊙ **High-Frequency Word,** *T38–T39*
New Word: *a* T

⊙ **Word and Picture Book,** *T39*

Leveled Reader

High-Frequency Word Practice, *T40*
Building Sentences

Vocabulary Reader

⊙ **Vocabulary Expansion,** *T41*
Using Position Words

Listening/Speaking/Viewing, *T41*

 Half-Day Kindergarten
Focus on lessons for tested skills marked with **T**. Then choose other activities as time allows.

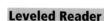

Target Skills of the Week

Phonemic Awareness	Onset and Rime; Initial Sound /h/; Blending Phonemes
Phonics	Initial Consonant: *H h*; Words with Short *a*
Comprehension	Text Organization and Summarizing; Question
Vocabulary	High-Frequency Words; Using Position Words
Fluency	Phonics Library; Word and Picture Book

DAY 3

Nat at Bat
by Elizabeth Kiley
illustrated by Holly Berry

Daily Routines, *T42-T43*
Calendar, Message, High-Frequency Words

Phonemic Awareness T

Reading the Big Book, *T44-T48*

Comprehension Skill, *T45, T46, T49*
Text Organization and Summarizing T

Concepts of Print, *T45*
Word Spacing T

Phonics, *T50*
Review Initial Consonant *h*; Blending Short *a* Words T

Reading Decodable Text, *T51-T53*
"Nat at Bat"

Vocabulary Reader

Leveled Reader

Building Words, *T54*
Words with Short *a*

Shared Writing, *T55*
Writing a Newsletter

DAY 4

We Read Together

Daily Routines, *T56-T57*
Calendar, Message, High-Frequency Words

Phonemic Awareness T

Reading the Social Studies Link, *T58-T59*

Comprehension Strategy, *T58*
Question

Comprehension Skill, *T58*
Text Organization and Summarizing T

Concepts of Print, *T59*
First Letter in a Written Word T

Phonics, *T60–T61*
Blending Short *a* Words T

Vocabulary Reader

Leveled Reader

Building Words, *T62*
Words with Short *a*

Interactive Writing, *T63*
Using Position Words

DAY 5

Daily Routines, *T64-T65*
Calendar, Message, High-Frequency Words

Phonemic Awareness T

Revisiting the Literature, *T66*

Comprehension Skill, *T66*
Text Organization and Summarizing T

Building Fluency, *T67*

Phonics Review, *T68*
Consonants, Short *a* Words T

High-Frequency Word Review, *T69*
Words: *I, see, my, like, a* T

Word and Picture Book, *T69*

Vocabulary Reader

Leveled Reader

Building Words, *T70*
Words with Short *a*

Independent Writing, *T71*
Journals: Recording Information

Concepts of Print lessons teach important foundational skills for Phonics.

Managing Flexible Groups

Leveled Instruction and Leveled Practice

	DAY 1	**DAY 2**
WHOLE CLASS	• Daily Routines (TE pp. T24–T25) • Teacher Read Aloud: *Friends at School* (TE pp. T26–T27) • Phonemic Awareness lesson (TE pp. T28–T29)	• Daily Routines (TE pp. T32–T33) • Big Book: *Aaron and Gayla's Alphabet Book* (TE pp. T34–T35) • Phonics lesson (TE pp. T36–T37) • High-Frequency Word lesson (TE pp. T38–T39)
SMALL GROUPS *Organize small groups according to children's needs.*	**TEACHER-LED GROUPS** • Begin Practice Book pp. 129, 130, 131, 132. (TE pp. T27, T29) • Introduce Phonics Center. (TE p. T29) • Leveled Reader	**TEACHER-LED GROUPS** • Begin Practice Book pp. 133, 134. (TE p. T37, T39) • Write letters *H, h*; begin handwriting Blackline Master 164 or 190. (TE p. T37) • Introduce Phonics Center. (TE p. T37) • Leveled Reader • Vocabulary Reader
	INDEPENDENT GROUPS • Complete Practice Book pp. 129, 130, 131, 132. (TE pp. T27, T29) • Use Phonics Center. (TE p. T29)	**INDEPENDENT GROUPS** • Complete Practice Book pp. 133, 134. (TE pp. T37, T39) • Complete Blackline Master 164 or 190. • Use Phonics Center. (TE p. T37) • **Fluency Practice** Reread Word and Picture Book: *I See a*  . (Practice Book pp. 215–216)

English Language Learners
Support is provided in the Reaching All Learners notes throughout the week.

Independent Activities

• Complete Practice Book pages 129–138.
• Complete penmanship practice (Teacher's Resouce Blackline Masters 164 or 190 and 157 or 183).
• Reread familiar Phonics Library or Word and Picture Book stories.
• Share trade books from Leveled Bibliography. (See pp. T4–T5)

DAY 3

- Daily Routines (TE pp. T42–T43)
- Big Book: *Aaron and Gayla's Alphabet Book* (TE pp. T44–T49)
- Phonics lesson (TE p. T50)

TEACHER-LED GROUPS

- Begin Practice Book pp. 135, 136. (TE pp. T49, T50)
- Write letters *A, a;* begin handwriting Blackline Master 157 or 183.
- Read Phonics Library: "Nat at Bat." (TE pp. T51–T53)
- Leveled Reader
- Vocabulary Reader

INDEPENDENT GROUPS

- Complete Practice Book pp. 135, 136. (TE pp. T49, T50)
- Complete Blackline Master 157 or 183.
- **Fluency Practice** Reread Phonics Library: "Nat at Bat." (TE pp. T51–T53)

DAY 4

- Daily Routines (TE pp. T56–T57)
- Social Studies Link: *We Read Together* (TE pp. T58–T59)
- Phonics lesson (TE pp. T60–T61)

TEACHER-LED GROUPS

- Begin Practice Book p. 137. (TE p. T61)
- Introduce the Phonics Center. (TE p. T61)
- **Fluency Practice** Reread Word and Picture Book: *I See a* [image] .
- Leveled Reader
- Vocabulary Reader

INDEPENDENT GROUPS

- Complete Practice Book p. 137. (TE p. T61)
- **Fluency Practice** Color and reread Phonics Library: "Nat at Bat." (TE pp. T51–T53)
- Use Phonics Center. (TE p. T61)

DAY 5

- Daily Routines (TE pp. T64–T65)
- Rereading (TE pp. T66–T67)
- Phonics and High-Frequency Word Review (TE pp. T68–T69)

TEACHER-LED GROUPS

- Begin Blackline Master 36 (TE p. T67)
- Read Word and Picture Book: *I Like* [image] .
- Begin Practice Book p. 138. (TE p. T69)
- **Fluency Practice** Reread the Take-Home version of "Nat at Bat."
- Leveled Reader
- Vocabulary Reader

INDEPENDENT GROUPS

- Complete Blackline Master 36 (TE p. T67)
- Complete Practice Book p. 138. (TE p. T69)
- **Fluency Practice** Reread Word and Picture Book *I Like* [image] . Reread a favorite Phonics Library or Leveled Reader story.

- Retell or reread Little Big Books.
- Listen to Big Book Audio CDs.
- Use the Phonics Center and other Centers. (See pp. T22–T23)

Turn the page for more independent activities.

Managing Flexible Groups

Classroom Management

Independent Activities

Assign these activities at any time during the week while you work with small groups.

Differentiated Instruction

- **Handbook for English Language Learners** pp. 114–123
- **Extra Support Handbook** pp. 110–119

Additional Independent Activities

- **Classroom Management Handbook**, pp. 74–81
- **Challenge Handbook**, pp. 26–27

★ **Look for more activities in the Classroom Management Kit.**

Setting Up Centers

ABC Phonics Center

Materials Phonics Center materials for Theme 4, Week 1

Children work with letters and their sounds this week. They also make words with the letters *h, s, m, r, t, b, n,* and short *a.* Prepare materials for the Days 1, 2, and 4 activities. Cut apart the letter grids and bag them in plastic by color. Put out the Workmats and open the Direction Chart to the appropriate day. Follow the **Phonics Center** Routine. See pages T29, T37, and T61 for this week's **Phonics Center** activities.

Book Center

Materials books about friends

In addition to the books listed in the Bibliography, put copies of classic favorites in the Book Center after you've read them aloud. Look for *Corduroy* by Don Freeman and *May I Bring a Friend?* by Beatrice Schenk de Regniers. Most children will not be able to read the books, but they never seem to tire of looking at the pictures.

Corduroy by Don Freeman
May I Bring a Friend? by Beatrice Schenk de Regniers
Little Bear's Friend by Else Holmelund Minarik

Writing Center

Materials crayons • markers • lined and unlined writing paper • blank books

To begin the theme, children draw pictures of things they do with friends. For many beginning kindergarteners, writing is drawing. Emergent writers should be encouraged to label their drawings. Put out stacks of paper, colorful markers, and an assortment of fat crayons. Each time you begin a theme, add something exciting to the Writing Center. Stamps, stickers, sponge letters, and letter templates can spark renewed interest in writing. See pages T31, T49, and T63 for this week's Writing Center activities.

Art Center

Materials drawing paper • crayons or paints • yarn pieces

Pairs of children draw portraits of each other for a bulletin board display. They also draw pictures of objects and label with position words. To make the Art Center routine easy to manage, label storage containers: *Crayons, Pencils, Erasers,* and so on. Build in sufficient center time for each group to tidy the area for the next group. See pages T35 and T41 for this week's Art Center activities.

DAY 1
week 1

Day at a Glance
T24–T31

Learning to Read
Teacher Read Aloud, *T26*
Phonemic Awareness: */h/, T28*

Word Work
High-Frequency Word Practice, *T30*

Writing & Oral Language
Oral Language, *T31*

Daily Routines

Calendar

Reading the Calendar
Point to and read the day and date on the calendar. Help children find and name the day *before* today. Say that we use the word *yesterday* to talk about the day before today. Listen for children to use *yesterday* in conversation.

Sunday	Monday	Tuesday	Wednesday	Thursday	Friday	Saturday
			1	2	3	4
5	6	7	8	9	10	11
12	13	14	15	16	17	18
19	20	21	22	23	24	25
26	27	28	29	30	31	

yesterday

Daily Message

Modeled Writing
Use *yesterday* in your daily message

Yesterday the guinea pig ate all his food.

Word Wall

High-Frequency Words Have children chant the spelling of each word on the Word Wall today. *I* spells *I* and *s-e-e* spells *see* and *m-y* spells *my* and *l-i-k-e* spells *like.*

I	my	see	like

Word Cards for these words appear on pages R8–R9.

Daily Phonemic Awareness

Blending and Segmenting Onset and Rime

- Read "My Teddy Bear" on page 18 of *Higglety Pigglety*. Then play a sound blending game. I'll say some sounds. You put them together to make words from the poem: /b/ . . . /ear/ (bear); /f/ . . . /ur/ (fur); /n/ . . . /eed/ (need). Continue with one-syllable words from the poem.

- Now have partners decide on a word. They separate the beginning sound from the rest of the word, and then they ask the rest of the class to blend the word.

Blending Phonemes

- We have said the first sound by itself and the rest of the word. Now I'll say every sound separately. You can put them together to make words: /c/ /ă/ /n/ (can); /n/ /ē/ /d/ (need); /m/ /ō/ /st/ (most).

- Continue with other one-syllable words from the poem.

My Teddy Bear

A teddy bear is a faithful friend.
You can pick him up at either end.
His fur is the color of breakfast toast,
And he's always there when you need him most.

18

***Higglety Pigglety: A Book of Rhymes*, page 18**

Getting Ready to Learn

To help children plan their day, tell them that they will–

- Listen to a story called *Friends at School*.

- meet a new Alphafriend.

- read and explore books about friends in the Book Center.

Read Aloud

Selection Summary

This photo essay explores a typical kindergarten day.

Key Concepts

School activities
School friends

Teacher Read Aloud

Building Background

Tell children that they'll hear a story called *Friends at School*.

- Read the author's name and the photographer's name. Explain that a photographer is a person who takes pictures with a camera.

- Preview the pages of the book and invite discussion by pointing out that it has photographs instead of pictures. Photos tell the reader that the book is about real children in a real classroom.

 COMPREHENSION STRATEGY

Question

Teacher Modeling Model the Question strategy as you share the title and a few illustrations.

> **Think Aloud** One good way to understand what I read is to ask myself questions. I'll ask: What will the children in this classroom do? Do we do things like this in our classroom?

 COMPREHENSION SKILL

Text Organization and Summarizing

Teacher Modeling Model how to get the main idea from the text.

> **Think Aloud** I know from the title that this story is about school. I wonder what kinds of things these children do in their classroom. Is it like our classroom? Is it different? Let's read to find out.

Listening to the Story

Read the story, stopping briefly to model the Question strategy. Encourage children's comments and questions.

Responding

Oral Language: Summarizing the Story Help children summarize parts of the story.

- What is this story mostly about?
- What are some things you like to read about? Think about what children did inside and outside the classroom.
- Which things do we do in our classroom? Which don't we do?

Oral Language: Literature Circle In small groups, use these prompts to get the discussion going:

- What did you like best about this book?
- Do you have a favorite picture? Tell why you like it.
- Would you like to go to the school in this book? Why or why not?
- Which of these children would you like to have for a friend? Why?

Class Book Children may wish to make a *Friends at School* class book.

Practice Book Children will complete **Practice Book** pages 129–130 during small group time.

Practice Book page 129

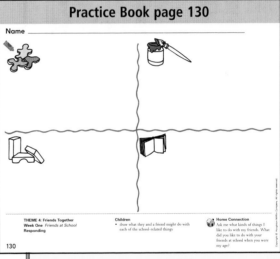

Practice Book page 130

Book Center

Fill your Book Center with books about friends. Include classics as well as newer titles like *May I Bring a Friend?* by Beatrice Schenk de Regniers, *Best Friends for Frances* by Russell Hoban, *The Very Lonely Firefly* by Eric Carle, *Friend Frog* by Alma Flor Ada, and *A Weekend with Wendell* by Kevin Henkes.

OBJECTIVES

- Identify pictures whose names begin with /h/.

Materials

- **Alphafriend Cards** *Benny Bear, Hattie Horse, Nyle Noodle*
- **Alphafriend CD** Theme 4
- **Alphafolder** *Hattie Horse*
- **Picture Cards** for *h, b,* and *n*
- **Phonics Center** Theme 4, Week 1, Day 1

Alphafolder *Hattie Horse*

Home Connection

Hand out the take-home version of Hattie Horse's Song. Ask children to share the song with their families. (See **Alphafriends Blackline Masters.**)

INSTRUCTION

PHONEMIC AWARENESS
Beginning Sound

❶ Teach

Introduce Alphafriend: Hattie Horse.
Use the Alphafriend routine to introduce Hattie Horse.

▶ **Alphafriend Riddle** Read these clues:

- Our new Alphafriend is an animal that lives on a farm.
- Her name is *Hhhattie.* Instead of feet, she has *hhhoofs* that go "Clip-clop."
- She has long *hhhair* called a *mane.* What animal is she?

When most hands are up, call on children until they say *horse.*

▶ **Pocket Chart** Display Hattie Horse in a pocket chart. Explain that Hattie's sound is /h/. Say her name, stretching the /h/ sound slightly, and have children echo this.

▶ **Alphafriend CD** Have children listen for /h/ words.

▶ **Alphafolder** Children name the /h/ pictures in the illustration.

▶ **Summarize**

- What is our Alphafriend's name? What is her sound?
- What words in our Alphafriends song start with /h/?
- Each time you look at Hattie this week, remember the /h/ sound.

Hattie Horse's Song

(tune: The Wheels on the Bus)

Hattie is a hungry horse.

She's hungry for her hay, of course.

Hattie is a hungry horse.

She hurries home at noon.

❷ Guided Practice

Listen for /h/ and compare and review /n/ and /b/. Add Alphafriends *Benny Bear* and *Nyle Noodle* to the pocket chart. Review each character's sound.

Hold up Picture Cards one at a time. Tell children they should signal "thumbs up" for words that start with Hattie Horse's sound, /h/. Have children put those cards below Hattie's picture. For "thumbs down" words, children put cards below the correct Alphafriends.

Pictures: *hat, hen, hose, net, nine, nut, bat, bell, bike.*

Tell children they will sort more pictures in the **Phonics Center** today.

❸ Apply

Children complete **Practice Book** pages 131–132 at small group time.

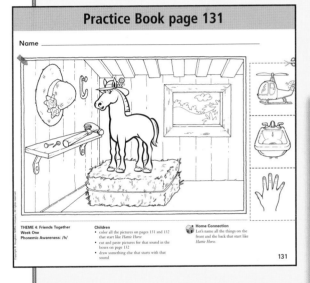

Practice Book page 131

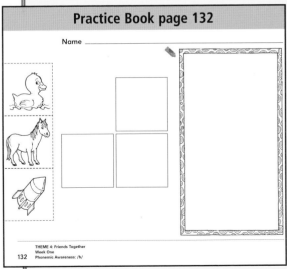

Practice Book page 132

ⒶⒷⒸ Phonics Center

Materials — Phonics Center materials for Theme 4, Week 1, Day 1 ·············

Display Day 1 Direction Chart. Children put *Hattie Horse, Benny Bear,* and *Nyle Noodle* (without letters) in separate sections of Workmat 3. Then they sort remaining pictures by initial sound: /b/, /h/, and /n/.

OBJECTIVES

- Read high-frequency words.
- Create and write sentences with high-frequency words.

Materials

- **Word Cards** *I, my, like*
- *Higglety Pigglety: A Book of Rhymes,* page 6
- **Picture Cards** *bike, cat, dog, desk*
- **Punctuation Card** period

High-Frequency Words

Display Word Cards for the high-frequency words *I, my,* and *like* in a pocket chart.

- Call on children to identify each word and to match it on the Word Wall.

- Remind children that these words are often found in books. I'll read a poem. You listen to hear if these words are used in it.

- Read the poem "Everybody Says." Did you hear any of these words in the poem? Let's see which **Word Cards** you can match to the words in the poem.

THEME 1

Everybody Says

Everybody says
I look just like my mother.
Everybody says
I'm the image of Aunt Bee.
Everybody says
My nose is like my father's.
But I want to look like ME!

by Dorothy Aldis

6

Higglety Pigglety: A Book of Rhymes, page 6

Have children write sentences.

- Tell children that they can write sentences with words they can now read. Model how to make the rebus sentences shown.

- Have writers make their own sentences with other **Picture Cards**. Some children will want to write new sentences and add their own rebuses. Children can use temporary phonics spelling to label their ideas.

| I | like | my | | • |

| I | like | my |  | |

ORAL LANGUAGE: VOCABULARY
Using Position Words

OBJECTIVES
● Use position words.
Materials
● Read Aloud *Friends at School*

❶ Teach

Display the book *Friends at School*.

● Let's look through this book again. I see Mocha *in* her pen. I see children *on* the floor. I see chairs *under* the puppet theater.

● Now who can find the grocery store? Where's the food? It's *on* the shelf. What about the money? Yes, it's *in* the cash register.

● Words like *in*, *on*, and *under* are important because they tell where things are.

● We use words like *in*, *on*, and *at* all the time when we talk with each other.

❷ Practice/ Apply

● Let's practice. Who can tell me what's *on* the table? *under* the table? *in* the tank?

on the table	under the table	in the tank
books markers paper	chair scraps	fish water rocks

Writing Center

Materials *Friends at School* • drawing paper • crayons

Display *Friends at School* in the Writing Center. Children think about their own classroom and draw favorite activities they do with their friends at school. Check their understanding of position words as they describe what they've drawn. If you are making a *Friends at School* Class Book, use children's illustrations from this activity.

English Language Learners

Model sentences demonstrating the meanings of the position words *in*, *on*, and *under*. Have children act them out. Then place objects in different positions, and have children use complete sentences to tell where the objects are.

Day at a Glance
T32–T41

Learning to Read

Big Book, *T34*

Phonics: Initial Consonant *h, T36*

High-Frequency Word *a, T38*

Word Work

High-Frequency Word Practice, *T40*

Writing & Oral Language

Vocabulary Expansion, *T41*

Daily Routines

Sunday	Monday	Tuesday	Wednesday	Thursday	Friday	Saturday
			1	2	3	4
5	6	7	8	9	10	11
12	13	14	15	16	17	18
19	20	21	22	23	24	25
26	27	28	29	30	31	

Calendar

Reading the Calendar To develop oral language facility, help children find and name the day after today. Say that we use the word *tomorrow* to talk about the day after today. Then listen for children using *tomorrow* in conversation.

Daily Message

Modeled Writing
Talk about the day after *today* by writing about an event that will happen *tomorrow*.

Today is Tuesday.
Tomorrow we will
carve a pumpkin.

Word Wall

High-Frequency Words Point to *I, see, my,* and *like* on the Word Wall. Have children read each word and use it in an oral sentence.

I	see	my	like

Word Cards for these words appear on pages R8–R9.

Daily Phonemic Awareness

Blending and Segmenting Onset and Rime

- Tell children that you are thinking of a position word and ask them to try to figure out what it is and to act it out.

- Say the word, segmenting it by onset and rime: /t//op/ (top); /l//eft/ (left); /b//ack/ (back). Then say the words one at a time.

- Call on individuals to segment each word by isolating the beginning sound and then saying the rest of the word.

Blending Phonemes

- Read "Humpty Dumpty" on page 19 of *Higglety Pigglety*.

- Now I'll say all the sounds in a word. You put them together to make a word from the poem: /s//ă//t/ (sat); /m//ĕ//n/ (men); /o//n/ (on).

- Continue the game with other one-syllable words.

Humpty Dumpty

Humpty Dumpty sat on a wall.
Humpty Dumpty had a great fall.
All the King's horses and
all the King's men
Couldn't put Humpty
together again.

a Mother Goose Rhyme

Higglety Pigglety: A Book of Rhymes, page 19

Getting Ready to Learn

To help children plan their day, tell them that they will—

- listen to a **Big Book:** *Aaron and Gayla's Alphabet Book*.

- learn the new letters *Hh*, and find words that begin with *h*.

- draw friends' pictures in the Art Center.

OBJECTIVES

- Introduce concepts of print.
- Develop story language.
- Reinforce comprehension strategy and comprehension skill.

Aaron and Gayla's Alphabet Book

Selection Summary Two friends share lots of fun—all the way from A to Z.

Key Concepts

The alphabet
Alphabetical order

INSTRUCTION

Reading the Big Book

Building Background

Ask children to name an alphabet book they've seen. You might briefly display some others. Then introduce *Aaron and Gayla's Alphabet Book*.

Read the title and the names of the author and the illustrator. Ask children to predict how this **Big Book** will be like other alphabet books.

COMPREHENSION STRATEGY
Question

Teacher Modeling Model the Question strategy as you read the title and point to the pictures.

Think Aloud Sometimes asking yourself questions as you read helps you to understand a book better. I wonder: Who are Aaron and Gayla? And what will they do with the alphabet? I'll look for answers as I read. As you listen, you do that, too.

COMPREHENSION SKILL
Text Organization and Summarizing

Teacher Modeling Children should understand that this book is organized by the alphabet. Model how knowing the alphabet helps the reader.

Think Aloud I know that this is an alphabet book. So as I read, I'm going to look at the letters. I'll think about things that begin with each letter. So knowing the alphabet will help me enjoy this book.

Big Book Read Aloud

Read the selection aloud, emphasizing that Aaron and Gayla do something for each letter of the alphabet. Track the print as you read. Pause frequently to encourage discussion.

Responding

Oral Language: Personal Response Have children choose their favorite scenes from the book. Use these prompts in the discussion.

• What did Aaron and Gayla do together? Do you do these things, too?

• What do you like to do with a friend? Why?

• What do you like to do by yourself? Why?

Art Center

Materials paper • crayons or paint • yarn pieces

Have pairs work to draw portraits of each other. Make a "Classroom Friends" bulletin board. Link the two friends' pictures with yarn.

Extra Support/ Intervention

Help children identify the letters of the alphabet by displaying an alphabet strip and providing magnetic letters for them to match and build their own alphabet.

PHONICS

WEEK 1

OBJECTIVES

- Identify words that begin with /h/.
- Identify pictures whose names begin with /h/.
- Write the letters *H, h.*

Materials

- **Alphafriend Cards** *Benny Bear, Hattie Horse, Nyle Noodle*
- **Letter Cards** *h, n,* and *b*
- **Picture Cards** *horse, hen, hose; net, nut, nose; bat, bell, bed*
- **Blackline Master** 164
- **Phonics Center** Theme 4, Week 1, Day 2

Hattie Horse's Song

(tune: The Wheels on the Bus)

Hattie is a hungry horse.

Hungry for her hay,
   of course.

Hattie is a hungry horse.

She hurries home at noon.

Extra Support/Intervention

To help children remember the sound for *h,* have them listen to the song for Hattie Horse in the Listening Center.

PHONICS
Initial Consonant *h*

❶ Phonemic Awareness Warm-Up

Beginning Sound Read or sing the lyrics to Hattie Horse's song, and have children echo it line-for-line. Have them listen for the /h/ words and raise their hands for each one. See Theme Resources page R2 for music and lyrics.

❷ Teach Phonics

Beginning Letter Display the *Hattie Horse* card, and have children name the letter. Say: The letter *h* stands for the sound /h/, as in *horse.* When you see an *h,* remember Hattie Horse. That will help you remember the sound /h/.

Write *horse* on the board. Underline the *h.* What is the first letter in the word *horse? Horse* starts with /h/, so *h* is the first letter I write for *horse.*

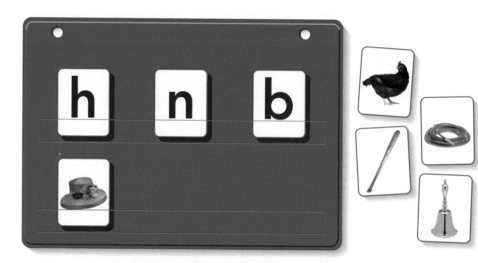

❸ Guided Practice

Compare and Review: *b, n* In a pocket chart, display the **Letter Cards** as shown and the **Picture Cards** in random order. Review the sounds for *h, n,* and *b.* In turn, children can name a picture, say the beginning sound, and put the card below the right letter. Tell children they will sort more pictures in the **Phonics Center** today.

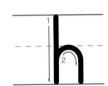

Handwriting Rhyme: H

Two tall lines standing
next to each other,
Connect them at
the middle.
They hold hands with
each other.

Handwriting Rhyme: h

One straight, tall line
And a curvy little bump
Makes a hook like
A little camel's hump.

Penmanship: Writing _H, h_ Tell children that now they'll learn to write the letters that stand for /h/: capital _H_ and small _h_. Write each letter as you recite the penmanship rhyme. Children can listen to the rhyme as they "write" the letter in the air.

④ Apply

Have children complete **Practice Book** page 133 at small group time.

For additional penmanship practice assign **Blackline Master** 164. Penmanship practice for the continuous stroke style is available on **Blackline Master** 190.

Practice Book page 133

ABC Phonics Center

Materials Phonics Center materials for Theme 4, Week 1, Day 2 . . . .

Display Day 2 Direction Chart. Children put _Hattie Horse, Nyle Noodle,_ and _Benny Bear_ (with letters) in separate sections of Workmat 3. Then they sort remaining pictures by initial letter: _h, b,_ and _n._

OBJECTIVES

- Read and write the high-frequency word *a*.

Materials

- **Word Cards** *I, see, a*
- **Picture Cards** *bat, box, dog, hat, horse, man*
- **Punctuation Card** period
- *Higglety Pigglety: A Book of Rhymes,* page 20

INSTRUCTION

HIGH-FREQUENCY WORD
New Word: *a*

❶ Teach

Introduce the word *a*. Tell children that today they'll learn to read and write a word that they will often see in stories. Say *a* and use it in oral context.

Gayla is *a* girl.　　　She has *a* friend.　　　They play with *a* ball.

- Write *a* on the board. Explain that this is a letter and a word, too.

- Have children echo a few phrases after you: *a bat, a horse, a car, a doll.*

- Ask children to answer some questions using the word. **What animal can fly?** (a bird) **What animal says "oink-oink"?** (a pig) **What do you read?** (a book)

Word Wall Explain that the capital letter, *A*, is used at the beginning of a sentence. Post *a* and *A* on the Word Wall, reminding children to look there when they need to remember how to write the word.

❷ Guided Practice

Build these sentences one at a time. Ask children to take turns reading the sentences.

- Place the pocket chart in the Writing Center for children to build more sentences.

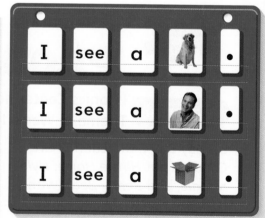

Display *Higglety Pigglety: A Book of Rhymes,* page 20.

- Reread the poem "Notice." Remind children that they've heard it before. This time they'll listen for their new word, *a.*

- Children indicate a "thumbs up" when they hear the word.

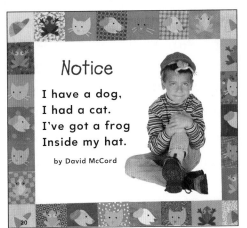

Higglety Pigglety: A Book of Rhymes, page 20

Practice Book pages 134

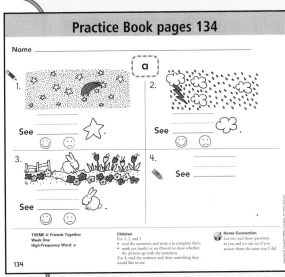

❸ Apply

- Children complete **Practice Book** page 134 at small group time.

- On Day 3, they will practice reading *a* in the **Phonics Library** story "Nat at Bat."

- Pass out copies of *I See a* 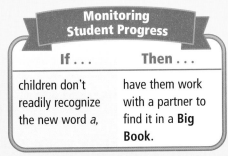 on **Practice Book** pages 215–216. Read the title aloud. Ask children to tell where this story takes place. Ask them where they think the playground is located.

For each page, have children look at the picture and tell what the boys and girls are doing. Have them read the page silently. Then ask a child to read the page aloud. Use questions such as the following to prompt discussion:

Pages 1–3 What do you see? What are the boys and girls doing in each picture?

Page 4 Did we guess where the playground was? Point to the sentence that tells you this.

Ask children to count the high-frequency words in the story: How many times can you find the word *I* in this story? the word *see?* the word *a?*

Practice Book pages 215–216

Monitoring Student Progress

If . . .	Then . . .
children don't readily recognize the new word *a,*	have them work with a partner to find it in a **Big Book**.

High-Frequency Words

OBJECTIVES

- Read high-frequency words.
- Create and write sentences with high-frequency words.

Materials

- **Word Cards** *I, see, a*
- **Picture Cards** *hat, hen, horse*
- **Punctuation Card** period

Tell children that you want to build a sentence about something you see.

- Play "I Spy" with **Picture Cards** *hat, horse,* and *hen.*
- Tell children that you'll make a sentence about something you "spied" on one of the cards.
- Display the **Word Cards** *I see* in the pocket chart, and read them.
- I want the next word to be *a.* Who can find *a* for me?
- Finish the sentence with a **Picture Card**. Ask children what mark goes at the end. Read the sentence together. Then have children read it alone.
- Children take turns building more sentences.

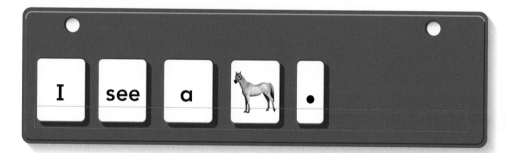

Have children write sentences.

- Have children write the sentence stem from above.
- Children can finish the sentence with a picture. Some children can label or write about what they've drawn. Explain that they can use temporary phonics spellings, saying the words slowly and writing the letters they hear.

VOCABULARY EXPANSION
Using Position Words

Listening/Speaking/Viewing

Discuss position words.

- Remind children that position words tell where someone or something is.
- Briefly review position words from a previous list.

Use Alphafriend *Hattie Horse* to demonstrate position words.

- Hold Hattie Horse beside, on, under, and over a ball or small object. Illustrate the words on a chart.
- Repeat with each position word, and have children describe where Hattie Horse is.

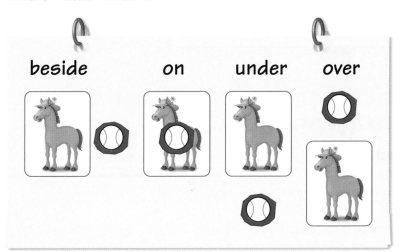

beside   on   under   over

Art Center

Materials   drawing paper • crayons or paints • yarn pieces

On the art table, place a small number of objects: a box, bag, pencil, marker, ball, apple, and book. Children place objects *in, under, beside,* and *over.* They draw a picture and use positions words to describe where the objects are.

beside the box

OBJECTIVES

- Use position words in an oral context.
- Learn academic language: *position words.*

Materials

- Alphafriend Card *Hattie Horse*

Vocabulary Support

The Vocabulary Reader can be used to develop and reinforce vocabulary related to the instruction for this week.

Vocabulary Reader

Where Is the Dog?
by Katherine James

VOCABULARY   WEEK 1

Day at a Glance

T42–T55

Learning to Read

Big Book, *T44*

Phonics: Reviewing Consonant *h*; Blending Short *a* Words, *T50*

Word Work

Building Words, *T54*

Writing & Oral Language

Shared Writing, *T55*

Daily Routines

Calendar

Sunday	Monday	Tuesday	Wednesday	Thursday	Friday	Saturday
			1	2	3	4
5	6	7	8	9	10	11
12	13	14	15	16	17	18
19	20	21	22	23	24	25
26	27	28	29	30	31	

Reading the Calendar Point to and read the day and date on the calendar. Review the concepts *yesterday, today,* and *tomorrow*.

Daily Message

Modeled Writing
Use some *h* words in today's message. As you write, ask: What sound do you hear first in *house?*

Harry has a new kitten in his house.

Word Wall

High-Frequency Words Choose a child to point to and read the two one-letter words: *I* and *a.* Then read all the words together.

I	a	see	my

Word Cards for these words appear on pages R8–R9.

Daily Phonemic Awareness

Blending and Segmenting Onset and Rime

- Play "Pat, Pat, Clap." Remind children how to pat their knees in a slow 2, 1 rhythm.

- Blend onset and rime in a slow rhythm: /c/ /at/, cat; /f/ /at/, fat.

Then give children the sounds, and have them blend the sounds to say the whole word on the clap beat.

- Next, whisper a word for an individual to segment into sounds. The rest of the class will then pat, pat the sounds and clap to say the word.

Blending Phonemes

- Now I'll say all the sounds in a word. You put them together to make the word. /f/ /ă/ /t/ (fat); /p/ /ĕ/ /t/ (pet); /w/ /ĭ/ /g/ (wig).

- Continue with the other words shown.

fat	pet	ten
met	Ben	wet
sit	nut	lit
cut	sun	bat
bun	win	run
pig	fun	wig

Getting Ready to Learn

To help children plan their day, tell them that they will–

- reread and talk about the **Big Book** *Aaron and Gayla's Alphabet Book*.

Aaron and Gayla's Alphabet Book
pictures by Jan Spivey Gilchrist
written by Eloise Greenfield
ABC

- read a story called "Nat at Bat."

Nat at Bat
by Elizabeth Kiley
illustrated by Holly Berry

- draw and write about something they like to do.

Rr
We ride.

Reading the Big Book

Aaron and Gayla's Alphabet Book

pictures by Jan Spivey Gilchrist
written by Eloise Greenfield

HOUGHTON MIFFLIN Reading

Includes:
Social Studies Link

Reading for Understanding

Reread *Aaron and Gayla's Alphabet Book*. Remind children that the book tells something for each letter of the alphabet. Pause for Comprehension points.

Aa My name is Aaron.

Bb I sit beside the window.

2

2

Cc I drive my car.

Dd I dig a hole.

4

Ee I eat my dinner.

Ff I look for a friend.

6

6

Extra Support/Intervention

To help children understand word spacing, have them place a finger between words in a sentence from the **Big Book** as you read the sentence aloud.

COMPREHENSION SKILL
Text Organization and Summarizing

pages 2–3

Teacher-Student Modeling Remind children that this book tells about something for each letter of the alphabet. Point to the letters on pages 2 and 3.

- I'll read the *Aa* page. Aaron's name is on this page, because it begins with *A*. What page comes next? How do you know?

REVISITING THE TEXT
Concepts of Print

page 13

Word Spacing

- Watch as I read. I can tell where one word stops and the next one begins by the space between the words. I'll put my finger in the space between the words. Now you try it.

- Have individuals follow your example.

COMPREHENSION SKILL

Text Organization and Summarizing

pages 14–15

Teacher-Student Modeling This page is about the letter *m*. How do we know what letter will come next? (*n*, because *n* follows *m* in the alphabet) **What did Aaron and Gayla do for the letter *n*?** (make noise)

CRITICAL THINKING

Guiding Comprehension

page 17

- **NOTING DETAILS** What game are Aaron and Gayla playing in this picture? How do you know? (hide and seek)

Oral Language

As you reread, point out the author's use of action words like *jump* and *run*. Ask children if they can think of other words Eloise Greenfield could have used, like *hop* and *skip*.

Ss We sit beside each other.

Tt We play together.

20

21

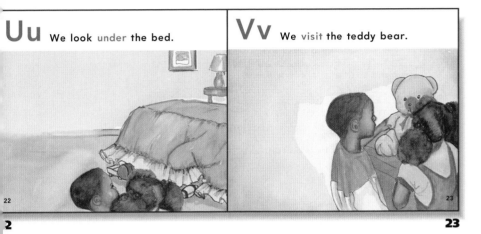

Uu We look under the bed.

Vv We visit the teddy bear.

22

23

Ww We play together.

Xx We x-ray the teddy bear.

24

25

CRITICAL THINKING
Guiding Comprehension

pages 22–25

- **SEQUENCE OF EVENTS** What do Aaron and Gayla do after they look under the bed? (visit the teddy bear)

- **SEQUENCE OF EVENTS** What do Aaron and Gayla do before they x-ray the teddy bear? (play together)

REACHING ALL LEARNERS

Challenge

Have children suggest alternate activities for selected letters of the alphabet. For example, Aaron and Gayla might *bike* for *b* or *hop* for *h*.

English Language Learners

Contrast *look for, look in,* and *look under.* Reread page 22, and have children act out what Aaron and Gayla are doing. Then reread pages 7, 10, and 13, and have children act out what the story characters are doing.

CRITICAL THINKING
Guiding Comprehension

pages 26–27

• **CAUSE/EFFECT** Why do you suppose Aaron and Gayla are yawning in this picture? What do you think they'll do next? (They're tired. They'll go to sleep.)

 **COMPREHENSION SKILL**
Text Organization and Summarizing

pages 2–27
Student Modeling Call on individuals to find different letters of the alphabet and to summarize what Gayla and/or Aaron did for each letter.

• Read the *B* page. On this page, I hear a *b* word, *beside.* I'll read the *S* page, and you tell me what the /s/ word is. (sit)

26

28

Responding

Oral Language: Retelling

Use these prompts to help children retell the story:

- What did Aaron and Gayla like to do together?
- Do you do any of these things with a friend?
- What kinds of things do you do when you play alone?

Practice Book Children will complete **Practice Book** page 135 during small group time.

Practice Book page 135

Writing Center

Have children draw something they like to do based on an alphabet letter. You might help by suggesting some activities. Children draw and label their illustrations.

Monitoring Student Progress

If . . .	Then . . .
children need more practice in understanding how alphabet books are organized,	make a display of a variety of alphabet books in the Book Center.

Responding **T49**

OBJECTIVES

- Identify words with initial consonant *h*, /h/.
- Blend and read words with *b, h, m, r, s, t,* and short *a*.
- Learn academic language: *vowel* or *helper letter.*

Materials

- **Alphafriend Cards** *Andy Apple, Hattie Horse*
- **Letter Cards** *a, b, h, m, r, s, t*
- **Alphafriend CD** Theme 4
- **Blending Routines Card 1**

Practice Book page 136

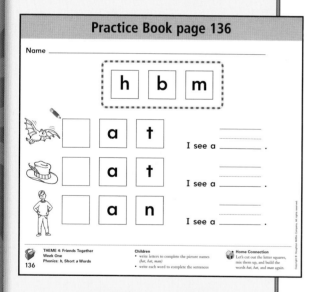

Name _____

h	b	m

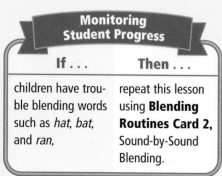

	a	t	I see a _____ .
	a	t	I see a _____ .
	a	n	I see a _____ .

THEME 4: Friends Together
Week One
Phonics: *h*, Short *a* Words
136

Children
- write letters to complete the picture names (*hat, hat, man*)
- write each word to complete the sentences

Home Connection
Let's cut out the letter squares, mix them up, and build the words *hat, hat,* and *man* again.

Monitoring Student Progress

If . . .	Then . . .
children have trouble blending words such as *hat, bat,* and *ran,*	repeat this lesson using **Blending Routines Card 2,** Sound-by-Sound Blending.

INSTRUCTION

TARGET SKILL
PHONICS
Blending Short *a* Words

❶ Teach: Connect Sounds to Letters

Review consonant *h*. Ask children what letter and sound they think of when they see Hattie Horse.

- Play Hattie Horse's song, and have children clap for each /h/ word.
- Write *H* and *h* on the board, and list words from the song.

Introduce short *a*. Tell children that they'll build a word with *h*, but first they'll learn about a vowel ("helper letter").

- Introduce Alphafriend *Andy Apple* and his song (music and lyrics, page R5). Say *Andy Apple* with me. Andy's letter is the vowel *a*, and the sound *a* usually stands for is /ă/.
- Hold up the **Letter Card** *a*. You say /ă/. Listen for the /ă/ sound in these words: /ă/ *apple*, /ă/ *ask*, /ă/ *after.*

Model Blending Routine 1. Show the **Letter Cards** *a* and *t*. Have children identify each letter and its sound.

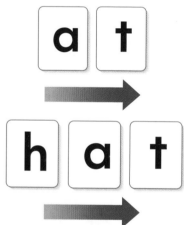

- Model blending the sounds as you point to each letter with a sweeping motion. I say the sounds in order: first /ă/, then /t/. I hold each sound until I say the next one, *ăăăt, at*. I've made the word *at*. Repeat, having children blend and pronounce *at* with you.
- Show **Letter Cards** *h, a, t*, and repeat with the word *hat, hhhăăăt, hat*. Repeat, having children blend *hat* on their own. Continue with *sat, bat,* and *rat.*

❷ Guided Practice

Check Understanding Display the word *mat* and ask individuals to blend the word. For more practice display *sat, ran*, and *man*. Have children blend the words, modeling blending as needed. Continue as children blend *ram, tab, Sam*. Have children read the sentence *I see my hat*, blending the sounds in *hat*. (Underlined words appear on the Word Wall.)

❸ Apply

Children complete **Practice Book** page 136 at small group time.

HOUGHTON MIFFLIN
Reading
Decodable Text

Phonics Library

Friends Together

Nat at Bat

by Elizabeth Kiley
illustrated by Holly Berry

1

PHONICS LIBRARY
Reading Decodable Text

Phonics/Decoding Strategy

Teacher-Student Modeling Discuss using the
Phonics/Decoding strategy to read words in the story.

Think Aloud Let's read the title. The first word begins with *N*.
The sound for *N* is /n/. The other letters are *a* and *t*.
I blend the letters to read this word: *NNNăăăt, Nat*. Then I see the
letters *a* and *t*. I can blend these letters to read the word: *ăăăt, at*.
The last word begins with *B*. The sound for *B* is /b/. The other letters
are *a* and *t*. I can blend these letters to read the word *băăăt*. I see
baseball players in the picture. Does the title "Nat at Bat" make
sense?

Preview the pictures on pages 2–3. Explain that Nat is a
name for a person or an animal. Ask children which player they
think is Nat. Ask: How do you think Nat is feeling?

OBJECTIVES

- Apply phonics skills to decode short *a* words.
- Apply high-frequency words.
- Reread for fluency practice.

Reading Decodable Text **T51**

Bat, Nat!

2

Nat sat.
My hat!

3

Prompts for Decoding

Have children read each page silently before reading aloud to you. Remind them to look at each letter as they sound out a word. Prompts:

page 2 Write the word *Nat* on the board. Model blending the sounds: *Nnnăăăt, Nat.* Remind children to hold each sound until they say the next one. Point out the comma in the sentence *Bat, Nat!* Tell children that when they see a comma, it is a signal to pause.

page 3 What word rhymes with *Nat?* What letters are the same in these words? Why do you think Nat is sitting down?

page 5 Nat is finally at bat! What did Nat's teammates do to get him to bat?

Word Key

Decodable words with short *a* _____

High-Frequency Words _____

Bat, bat, bat, Nat!
Nat sat, sat, sat.

4

See Nat at bat!

5

Oral Language

Discuss the story. Remind children to speak in complete sentences.

- Look at the pictures. What does the team need to play baseball? (bat, baseball, mitts, bases)

- Why do you think Nat didn't want to play baseball? (He didn't think he was a very good baseball player.)

- How do you think Nat felt at the end of the story? (Very good. His friends helped him learn to bat.)

Identify rhyming words. Ask children to reread the story and identify rhyming words. (Nat, bat, sat) Then ask children to model blending these words. Have them think of any other words that rhyme with the ones they have found.

Build Fluency

Model fluent reading.

- Read aloud page 5. Then have children read the page aloud.

- Have children reread the same page several times until each child can read it aloud smoothly.

 Home Connection

Have children color the pictures in the take-home version of "Nat at Bat." After rereading on Day 4, they can take it home to read to family members. (See **Phonics Library Blackline Masters**.)

 Extra Support/Intervention

Read "Humpty Dumpty" on page 19 of **Higglety Pigglety: A Book of Rhymes.** Children name the words that start with /h/ and point to them on the page.

Reading Decodable Text **T53**

PRACTICE

BUILDING WORDS
Words with Short *a*

Model building the word *at*.

- Display **Letter Cards** *a, b, h, m, n, r, s, t*.

- Say: Listen to the word *at*. I'll say the sounds slowly, and we can build the word together: /ă/ /t/. How many sounds do you hear? The first sound is /ă/. What letter stands for /ă/?

- Put the **Letter Card** *a* in the chart. The next sound is /t/. What letter should I use? Add **Letter Card** *t* next to the *a*. That's the word *at*.

Model building words that rhyme with *at*.

- Now let's build the word *hat*, hhhăăăt. How many sounds do you hear? The first sound is /h/. What letter stands for /h/? Put the **Letter Card** *h* in the chart.

- The next sound is /ă/. What letter should I use? What is the last sound in *hat*? What letter should I use?

- Now what happens if I change /h/ to /s/? Continue making and blending short *a* words by substituting *m, r, s,* and *b* for the first letter.

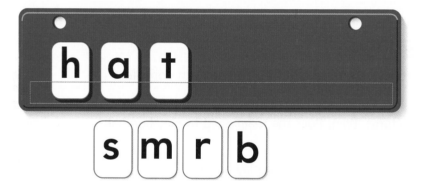

Word Wall Add *at* to the Word Wall. Have a child point to the word *at*. Remind children that they can use *at* to help them read and write words that rhyme with *at*.

Check Understanding Have children use magnetic letters or other manipulatives from your collection to build the word *bat*. Show them how to make needed corrections. Have individuals model blending the word.

Extend Practice Continue the above procedure, mixing spelling patterns by building these words: *tan, bat, sat, tab, ham, Nat, man*. Display this sentence: *I like my hat*. Tell children to read the underlined words (found on the Word Wall) without sounding them out and to blend the other word to read the sentence.

SHARED WRITING
Writing a Newsletter

OBJECTIVES
• Use position words in an oral context.
• Participate in shared writing.

Review position words.

• Have children tell each other about the position word drawings they made in the Art Center yesterday. (See page T41.)

• Tell children they'll write a newsletter about things they do at school.

Use a graphic organizer to prepare to write.

• On chart paper, begin a graphic organizer such as the one below.

• As children stand at their favorite work stations, use position words to describe what you see.

• As you write, point out the spaces between words, and appropriate capitalization and punctuation.

• Children complete an *I like to* sentence stem. Put the sentences together with illustrations to make a newsletter to send home.

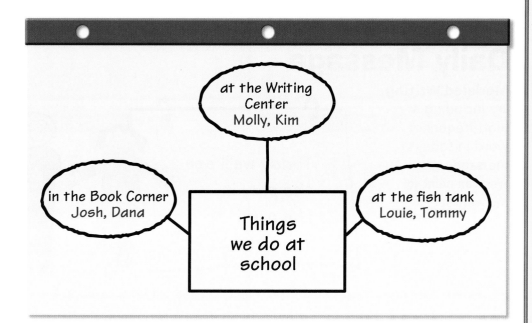

I like to write.   Molly

I like to read.   Josh

 English Language Learners

Work with English language learners and the completed graphic organizer as a group. Help children practice combining a classmate's name with *is* and a prepositional phrase to make a complete sentence, such as: *Josh is in the Book Corner.*

DAY 4
week 1

Day at a Glance
T56–T63

Learning to Read

Big Book, *T58*

Phonics: Reviewing Consonant *h*; **Blending Short** *a* **Words,** *T60*

Word Work

Building Words, *T61*

Writing & Oral Language

Interactive Writing, *T63*

Daily Routines

Sunday	Monday	Tuesday	Wednesday	Thursday	Friday	Saturday
			1	2	3	4
5	6	7	8	9	10	11
12	13	14	15	16	17	18
19	20	21	22	23	24	25
26	27	28	29	30	31	

Calendar

Reading the Calendar Point to today's date on the calendar. Say the day's name and point out that each day of the week is written with a capital letter. Point to yesterday's date. Ask: Who can point to the capital letter at the beginning of this day's name?

Daily Message

Modeled Writing Try including a high-frequency word in today's message. Ask: Who can point to the word *see*?

Today we'll <u>see</u> the play in the gym.

Word Wall

High-Frequency Words Clap and chant the words on the Word Wall. Pay special attention to the new word *a*.

a	my	like	see

Word Cards for these words appear on pages R8–R9.

Daily Phonemic Awareness

Blending and Segmenting Onset and Rime

- Reread "My Teddy Bear" on page 18 of *Higglety Pigglety*.

- Let's put some sounds together to make words from the poem: /c/ /an/ (can); /h/ /im/ (him); /m/ /ost/ (most).

- This time, I will say a word from the poem and you tell me the beginning sound and the rest of the word.

Blending Phonemes

- Now I'll say all the separate sounds in a word. You put them together to make a word from the poem: /ĭ/ /z/ (is); /p/ /ĭ/ /k/ (pick); /w/ /ĕ/ /n/ (when).

- Repeat with other single-syllable words from the poem.

My Teddy Bear

A teddy bear is a faithful friend.
You can pick him up at either end.
His fur is the color of breakfast toast,
And he's always there when you need him most.

18

Higglety Pigglety: A Book of Rhymes, page 18

Getting Ready to Learn

To help children plan their day, tell them that they will—

- read the Social Studies Link: *We Read Together*.

- read words in the **Phonics Center**.

- read a book called "Nat at Bat."

Nat at Bat
by Elizabeth Kiley
illustrated by Holly Berry

OBJECTIVES

- Tell how an article is organized.
- Identify the first letter of a written word.

Big Book

We Read Together

Social Studies Link

Aaron and Gayla's Alphabet Book

pictures by Jan Spivey Gilchrist
written by Eloise Greenfield

ABC

READING THE BIG BOOK
Social Studies Link

Building Background

Tell children that words carry important information. Ask what important information a traffic sign tells. A grocery list? An invitation?

Reading for Understanding Tell children that you'll read an article about children reading. Read the title, *We Read Together*. Then show a few pictures, and ask children what they think the article will be about.

COMPREHENSION STRATEGY
Question

Student Modeling Remind children to ask themselves questions as they read. Say, I wonder what this boy is reading. Who's he reading with?

COMPREHENSION SKILL
Text Organization and Summarizing

Student Modeling Remind children that *Aaron and Gayla's Alphabet Book* was organized by the alphabet. This article is organized differently. It's not an alphabet book.

Browse through the photographs before you read. What are all the children doing? How do you think this book will be organized? How will the pictures help you know?

Oral Language

menu: A menu is a list of foods you can order in a restaurant. Tell us about any menus you have seen. Did it have pictures or just words? How did the pictures help you?

English Language Learners

Bring a variety of printed materials—magazines, newspapers, menus, brochures, books, food labels—for children to examine. Talk about how writing is used in each. Then look for similar materials as you page through the book.

We read a grocery list.

32

We read a magazine.

33

We read a newspaper.

34

We read a menu.

35

We read a book . . .

36

by Eloise Greenfield.
And here she is!

37

CRITICAL THINKING
Guiding Comprehension

page 34

- **NOTING DETAILS** What part of the newspaper are they reading? How can you tell?

page 35

- **MAKING PREDICTIONS** What do you think the people in the picture might order? How do you know?

TARGET SKILL

REVISITING THE TEXT

Concepts of Print

page 34

First Letter in a Written Word

- Frame the sentence *We read a newspaper*. Have a child count the words.
- Frame the word *We*. Tell children that capital *W* is the first letter.
- Ask individuals to name the first letters in *read* and *newspaper*.

Responding

Oral Language: Summarizing Talk about the selection's main points. Then have children tell about their favorite parts, using pictures as prompts. Model rewording children's contributions as complete sentences if necessary.

REACHING ALL LEARNERS

Challenge

Have children choose books they can read and read them to friends.

OBJECTIVES

- Identify initial *h* for words that begin with /h/.
- Blend and read words with consonants and short *a*.

Materials

- *From Apples to Zebras: A Book of ABC's,* page 9
- **Alphafriend Cards** *Andy Apple, Hattie Horse*
- **Letter Cards** *a, b, h, m, N, r, s, S, t*
- **Picture Cards** *mat, bat, hat*
- **Phonics Center** Theme 4, Week 1, Day 4
- **Blending Routines Card 1**

PHONICS
Blending Short *a* Words

Review consonant *h*. Cover the words on page 9 of *From Apples to Zebras: A Book of ABC's.*

- Have children name the pictures.
- Ask what letter they expect to see first in each word. Uncover the words to confirm the predictions.

Review short *a*. Tell children that every word needs a vowel ("helper letter").

- Display Andy Apple and say his sound, /ă/.
- Have children suggest other words that start with /ă/. *(act, alligator, at, after, Alice)*

Review Blending Routine 1. Hold up **Letter Cards** *a* and *t*.

- Model blending the word *at*: /ă/, /t/, *ăăăt, at.*
- Put the **Letter Card** *h* in front of *at*. What happens when I add *h*? /h/ /ă/ /t/, *hhhăăăt, hat.*
- Continue, having individuals build and blend *bat, mat, Nat,* and *sat.*

Check Understanding Display the word *sat* and ask individuals to blend the word. For more practice display *man, rat,* and *ran* and have children blend the words, modeling blending as needed. Remind children to hold each sound until they say the next one, *mmmăăăn.* Continue as children blend the following: *ham, Sam, Nat.* Display the sentence *I like my hat.* Children should recognize the underlined words from the Word Wall. Tell them to blend the other word to read the sentence.

Hh

HOSPITAL

H

horse | hospital
hat | horn

9

From Apples to Zebras: A Book of ABC's, page 9

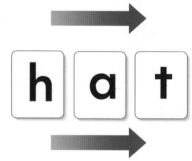

a | t

h | a | t

Home Connection

At home, children can look for grocery items or advertisements that begin with the /h/ sound. They draw pictures to share their discoveries.

T60 **THEME 4: Friends Together**

Practice/Apply In a pocket chart, display the **Picture Card** *mat*.

Have children say *mat* with you, stretching out the sounds slightly,

Then ask children to build *mat, bat,* and *hat*.

Children complete **Practice Book** page 137 at small group time.

In groups today, children will read short *a* words as they reread the **Phonics Library** story "Nat at Bat." See suggestions, pages T51–T53.

Practice Book page 137

Name _____

s	a	t	_____
r	a	n	_____
b	a	t	_____

A cat _____ .

A fat rat _____ .

I see Nat at _____ .

THEME 4: Friends Together
Week One
Phonics: Short *a* Words

Children
• add letters to build *sat, ran,* and *bat*
• write each word to complete the sentences

Home Connection
Would you like to listen to me read the words and sentences on this page? Then we can make up some other short *a* words.

137

ABC Phonics Center

Materials Phonics Center materials for Theme 4, Week 1, Day 4 ....

Display Day 4 Direction Chart and Workmat 4. Children place a **Picture Card** (*mat, bat,* or *hat*) in the first box and then build the word with **Letter Cards**, sound by sound. In the same way they build the other short *a* words.

Monitoring Student Progress

If . . .	Then . . .
children have trouble building words and sentences,	have them work with you or a partner.
children can easily build words and sentences,	have them create original sentences with short *a* words and have partners read them.

Phonics **T61**

- Blend consonant sounds with short *a* to read words.

- Letter Cards *a, b, h, m, N, s, S, r, t*

BUILDING WORDS
Words with Short *a*

Model building the word *at*.

- Display **Letter Cards** *a, b, h, m, n, r, s,* and *t*.

- Model how to build *at* in a pocket chart. Have children listen to the word *at*. **How many sounds do you hear? The first sound is /ă/. I'll put up an** *a* **to spell that. The last sound is /t/. What letter stands for that sound?** Add the letter *t* to the chart. Read the word together.

- Now I'll build *hat*. What letter do I need? Have a child add the **Letter Card** *h*.

- Build *bat, mat,* and *sat* next. Have children blend each word.

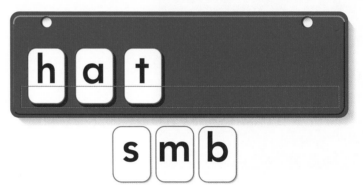

Check Understanding Small groups can work together to build short *a* words with magnetic letters or other manipulatives in your collection. Ask children to build *bat*. Provide corrections as needed. Then have them build other words and read them.

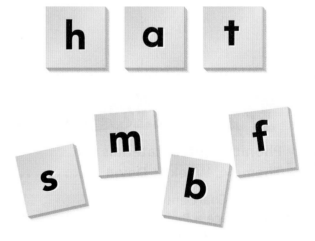

Extend Practice Continue the activity with *Sam, nab, ham,* and *man*. Exaggerate the final sound in each word to help children name the correct final consonant. Display the sentence *I see a hat*. Children should recognize the underlined words from the Word Wall. Tell them to blend the other word to read the sentence.

INTERACTIVE WRITING
Using Position Words

Use position words to write a description.

- Reread yesterday's Shared Writing activity. (See page T55.) Remind children that position words tell where someone or something is.

- Have a few children stand in different places around the room. Who is standing *beside* the bookshelf? Who is *under* the loft?

- Then write a short description of each person's position. Invite children to contribute to the writing by adding their names or a word they can write.

> Position Words
> I see Joe <u>under</u> the loft.
> Tom is <u>beside</u> the bookshelf.
> Mrs. Wilson is <u>at</u> the door.

Writing Center

Have children draw pictures of themselves in their favorite classroom center.

Put the chart paper from the previous activity in the Writing Center. Children might use the words to label their pictures.

English Language Learners

Have children perform actions relating to the prepositions *in, on, under,* and *beside,* such as: *Jana, please sit beside Mario,* or *Raul, please put this chalk on the desk.* Immediately ask about each action: *Where is Jana? Where is the chalk?*

Day at a Glance
T64–T71

Learning to Read

Revisiting the Literature, *T66*
Phonics: Review Consonants *b,* *n, h;* **Short** *a* **Words,** *T68*

Word Work

Building Words, *T70*

Writing & Oral Language

Independent Writing, *T71*

Daily Routines

Calendar

Reading the Calendar

Choose a child to tell today's date. Another child can point t● and tell what day of the week yesterday was. Ask: **What day wi** **tomorrow be?**

Sunday	Monday	Tuesday	Wednesday	Thursday	Friday	Saturday
			1	2	3	4
5	6	7	8	9	10	11
12	13	14	15	16	17	18
19	20	21	22	23	24	25
26	27	28	29	30	31	

Daily Message

Modeled Writing
Include some words that begin with *m, s, r, b* in today's message, to review beginning consonants and their sounds. Ask: **Who can point to a word that begins with** *m*? **with** *b*? **with capital** *M*?

> Today, Mike's mom will help us bake cookies for a snack.

Word Wall

High-Frequency Words Read the Word Wall together. Then play a rhyming game: I'm going to find a word that rhymes with *pat. At* rhymes with *pat.* Here's another word: *bike.* Raise your hand when you find a word that rhymes with *bike.*

a	to	like	me

Word Cards for these words appear on pages R8–R9.

Daily Phonemic Awareness

Blending and Segmenting Onset and Rime

- Read "Notice" on page 20 of *Higglety Pigglety*. Then play a guessing game. *Let's put sounds together to make words from the poem: /d/ /og/ (dog); /k/ /at/ (cat); /g/ /ot/ (got); /h/ /at/ (hat).*

- Now I will say a word from the poem and you tell me the beginning sound and the rest of the word.

Blending Phonemes

- *This time I will say all the separate sounds in a word. Raise your hand when you know it /d/ /ŏ/ /g/. That's right! /d/ /ŏ/ /g/,* dog. If children say *dig* or *dug*, repeat the sounds, emphasizing the one children need to hear to correct their mistake: ŏ.

- Continue with other words from the poem.

Higglety Pigglety: A Book of Rhymes, page 20

Getting Ready to Learn

To help children plan their day, tell them that they will—

- reread and talk about all the books they've read this week.

- take home a story they can read.

- write in their journals.

OBJECTIVES

● Review the week's selections.

REVISITING THE LITERATURE
Literature Discussion

Review the week's selections, using these suggestions.

● Choose a child to point out and describe a favorite classroom activity from *Friends at School*.

● Read pages 3 and 15 (*B* and *N* pages) of *Aaron and Gayla's Alphabet Book*, emphasizing the initial sound of each red word. Children can name the letter to which the page refers.

● Have partners retell *We Read Together*, using the pictures as clues.

● Together, reread "Nat at Bat." Call on individuals to model blending a word.

● Have children vote for a favorite book of the week. Graph the results of the voting. Then read the winning book aloud.

COMPREHENSION SKILL
Text Organization and Summarizing

Compare Books Ask children to talk about how the alphabet was important to *Aaron and Gayla's Alphabet Book*. Ask what each photograph in *We Read Together* showed. Choose a child to retell "Nat at Bat" in his or her own words

Rereading for Fluency

Reread Familiar Texts Remind children that they've learned the word *a* this week and that they've learned to read short *a* words. As children reread the **Phonics Library** story "Nat at Bat," have them find short *a* words.

- Feature several **Phonics Library** titles in the Book Corner. Have children demonstrate their growing skills by choosing one to reread aloud.

- Children can alternate pages with a partner. From time to time, ask children to point out words or pages that they can read more easily now.

Oral Reading and Retelling Stories Frequent rereadings of familiar texts help children develop a more expressive style in their oral reading. Model how to read in an enthusiastic tone, pausing for end punctuation. Then have children try it. Children can also practice retelling stories from earlier themes.

Nat at Bat
by Elizabeth Kiley
illustrated by Holly Berry

Cat's Surprise
by Susan Gorman-Howe
illustrated by Valeri Gorbachev

Baby Bear's Family
by Susan Gorman-Howe
illustrated by Angela Jarecki

Assign Blackline Master 36. Children can take it home to share their reading progress. A copy appears on page R12.

My Reading Log

I can read

My new words

a   hat

Books for Small-Group Reading

The materials listed below provide reading practice for children at different levels.

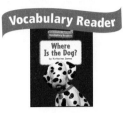

Vocabulary Reader

Where Is the Dog?

Leveled Reader

We Like To Play!

Little Big Book

Aaron and Gayla's Alphabet Book

Little Readers for Guided Reading

Houghton Mifflin Classroom Bookshelf

Home Connection

Remind children to share the take-home version of "Nat at Bat" with their families.

OBJECTIVES

- Build and read short *a* words.
- Make sentences with high-frequency words.

Materials

- **Word Cards** *I, see, my, like, a*
- **Picture Cards** for sentence building
- **Punctuation Card** period

PHONICS
Consonants, Short *a* Words

❶ Review

Review building short *a* words. Tell children that they will take turns being Word Builders and Word Readers. Have the Word Builders stand with you at the board.

- Let's write *at*. First, count the sounds. I know *a* stands for /ă/ and *t* stands for /t/. Let's write the letters on the board.

- Word Builders copy *at* from the board and blend the sounds.

- Add *h* in front of your letters. Word Builders write *hat* and ask the rest of the class (Word Readers) what new word they've made.

- A new group changes places with the first one. At your directions, they erase the *h* and write *b*. Then ask the Word Readers to say the new word.

- Continue until everyone builds a word by replacing one letter.

- Extend the activity by having Word Builders replace the final letter to make *ham, tab,* or *Sam.*

hat mat

HIGH-FREQUENCY WORDS
I, see, my, like, a

❷ Review

Review the high-frequency words.

- Ask children to identify the words *I, see, my, like,* and *a* on the Word Wall.

- Give each small group the **Word Cards, Picture Cards,** and **Punctuation Card** needed to make a sentence. Each child holds one card. Children stand and arrange themselves to make a sentence for others to read.

❸ Practice/Apply

- Children can complete **Practice Book** page 138 independently and read it to you during small group time.

- Pass out copies of **Practice Book** pages 217–218, *I Like* 🌈. Read the title aloud. Ask children to tell who is speaking. (the girl)

For each page, have children look at the picture and tell what the child sees. Have them read the page silently. Then ask an individual to read the page aloud. Use questions such as the following to prompt discussion:

Pages 1–3 What is the weather like in this story? How do you know? How does the girl feel about rainy days?

Page 4 What does the girl see now? Have you ever seen a rainbow? What colors did you see?

Then have children count the high-frequency words in the story: How many times can you find the word *I* in this story? the word *see?* the word *like?* the word *a?*

- Children can practice reading high-frequency words and decodable words by rereading the **Phonics Library** story "Nat at Bat."

Practice Book page 138

Practice Book pages 217–218

Monitoring Student Progress

If . . .	Then . . .
children need help remembering initial sounds,	show how many letters' names give clues to their sounds (*b,* /b/).
children pause at high-frequency words while reading,	have partners use **Word Cards** to practice high-frequency words.

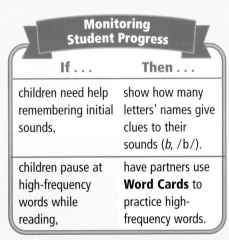

High-Frequency Words **T69**

OBJECTIVES

- Blend consonants with short *a* to read words.

Materials

- Letter Cards *a, b, h, m, n, r, s, t*

BUILDING WORDS
Words with Short *a*

Model building the word *at*.

- Remind children to hold each sound until they say the next one.

- Along the bottom of a pocket chart, line up the letters *s, m, r, b,* and *h*.

- Let's build the word *sat*, săăăt. Who can tell me which letter I should add to make *sat*? Choose a child to take the letter *s* and place it in front of *at*.

- Continue with *m, r, b,* and *h*. On chart paper, keep a list of all the short *a* words you make, and reread the list together.

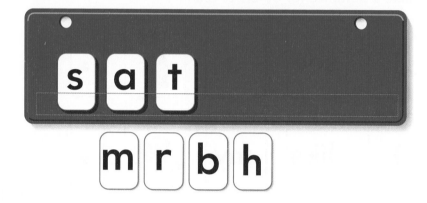

Check Understanding

Have small groups work together to build short *a* words with magnetic letters or other manipulatives. First have them build *mat* and *bat*. Provide corrections as needed. This time, children can add new words  to the Word Bank section of their journals and add appropriate pictures.

Extend Practice Continue building words using *ran, Sam, man,* and *tab*. Have children blend the words. Model blending as needed. Display the sentence *I see my hat*. Children should recognize the underlined words from the Word Wall. Tell them to blend the other word to read the sentence.

INDEPENDENT WRITING
Journals

Preparing to Write

● Journal writing should be independent. Provide plain paper for student journals to accommodate those children who are not ready for writing on lined paper, as well as for those who will be drawing as much as writing in their journals.

Writing Independently

● If children need a good idea to get started, you could suggest that they draw and label an activity they enjoyed during the week.

● You might also recommend they illustrate and label a scene from a book they read during the week.

● Remind children to use position words in their writing. They can use words on charts in the Writing Center, or they can say words slowly, writing the letters they hear.

Portfolio Opportunity

Mark journal entries you would like to share with parents. Allow children to mark their best efforts or favorite works for sharing as well.

 English Language Learners

Encourage English language learners to write about something they enjoyed learning or reading about in this theme. If necessary, give suggestions about drawing a special friend, a game they play at recess, or their favorite place in the classroom.

Leveled Readers

We Like To Play!
by Nicolas Thilo

We Like to Play!

Summary: *This nonfiction book describes a variety of activities children enjoy. Groups of active children are photographed riding, climbing, sliding, running, jumping, swinging, and playing.*

Story Words

We *p. 2*

to *p. 2*

play *p. 8*

High-Frequency Word

Review Word

like *p. 2*

Building Background and Vocabulary

Tell children that this story is about many different ways that children enjoy playing outdoors. Preview the photographs with children. Encourage children to share their own ideas about the kinds of outdoor activities they enjoy.

Comprehension Skill: Text Organization and Summarizing

Read together the Strategy Focus on the book flap and remind children to use the strategy as they read the story. Also tell children to use the title and the pictures to help them think about how the children in the story like to play. Have children read to find out the different ways the children in the story like to play.

Responding

Discussing the Book Have children share their personal responses to the book by encouraging them to talk about what they liked best about the story or what they found the most interesting. Have children point to sentences or photographs they enjoyed. Ask children to compare their favorite outdoor activities to the ones described in the story. What do children enjoy playing outdoors? Make a class list.

Responding Help children answer the questions on the inside back cover. Then work with them to complete the Writing and Drawing activity. Have children take turns sharing their drawings with classmates and explaining why they like the outdoor activity shown in the picture. Display all the pictures on a classroom bulletin board.

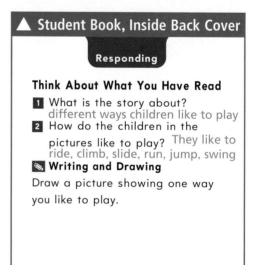

▲ Student Book, Inside Back Cover

Responding

Think About What You Have Read

1 What is the story about?
different ways children like to play
2 How do the children in the pictures like to play? They like to ride, climb, slide, run, jump, swing

✎ **Writing and Drawing**

Draw a picture showing one way you like to play.

Building Fluency

Model Reread pages 2 and 3 as children follow along in their books. Point out that the first three words, *We like to*, on the two pages are the same. Tell children that these words begin every page in the book.

Practice Have children reread the same two pages several times until each child can read it aloud smoothly. Then invite children to take turns reading aloud their favorite pages in the book.

Oral Language Development

Action Words Discuss action words with children. Explain that action words are words that name each action described in the story. Have children page through the story, pointing to the action word on each page (*ride, climb, slide, run, jump, swing*). After they find each word on a page, have them look at the photograph that shows that action.

Practice Ask volunteers to pantomime each action described in the book as you reread the book aloud.

High-Frequency Word
Review Word: *like*

Display the Word Card for *like*. Ask children to spell the word as you point to the letters. Then have children turn to page 8 in the book. Ask them to listen for the word *like* as you read *We like to play*. Ask children to take turns reading the sentence.

like

Lesson Overview

HOUGHTON MIFFLIN
Reading

My Dad and I

by Julio Ricardo Baerga
illustrated by Joe Cepeda

Includes:
Social Studies Link

Selection Summary

Through a series of shared activities—
playing soccer, drawing, singing—Rafa
and his dad show how they are very best
friends.

1 Teacher Read Aloud

• *The Lion and the Mouse*

2 Big Book

• *My Dad and I*
Genre: Realistic
Fiction

3 Decodable Text

Phonics Library

• "A Vat"

A Vat
by Elizabeth Kiley
illustrated by Bob Kolar

4 Social Studies Link

Friends
Help Friends

This Link appears after the main
Big Book selection.

Leveled Books

Vocabulary Reader

- Below Level, ELL
- Lesson
- Take-Home Version

Leveled Reader

- On Level, Above Level
- Lesson
- Take-Home Version

Instructional Support

Planning and Practice

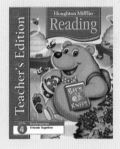

- Planning and Classroom Management
- Reading and skill instruction
- Plans and activities for reaching all learners

- Newsletters
- Observation Checklists
- Theme Activity Masters

- Phonemic Awareness
- Letter Recognition
- Phonics Practice

- Independent practice for skills
- Fluency Practice: Word and Picture Books

- Phonics Practice
- Word Building

Reaching All Learners

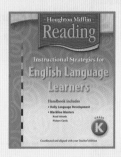

Coordinated lessons, activities, and projects for additional reading instruction for

- Classroom Teacher
- Extended Day
- Pull Out
- Resource Teacher

Technology

 Audio Selection

My Dad and I

Curious George Learns Phonics

www.eduplace.com

Daily Lesson Plans

T Skill tested on Weekly or Theme Skills Test and/or Integrated Theme Test

 60–90 minutes

WEEK 2 — DAILY LESSON PLANS

Learning to Read

Phonemic Awareness

Phonics

High-Frequency Words

Comprehension

Concepts of Print

 **Vocabulary Reader**
What Can You Do?

 Friends

Leveled Reader

 30–45 minutes

Word Work

High-Frequency Word Practice

Building Words

30–45 minutes

Writing and Oral Language

Vocabulary

Writing

Listening/Speaking/Viewing

DAY 1

Daily Routines, *T80–T81*
Calendar, Message, High-Frequency Words

⏱ **Phonemic Awareness** T

Teacher Read Aloud, *T82–T85*

⏱ **Comprehension Strategy,** *T82*
Predict/Infer

⏱ **Comprehension Skill,** *T82*
Cause and Effect **T**

⏱ **Phonemic Awareness,** *T86–T87*
Beginning Sound /v/ **T**

Leveled Reader

High-Frequency Word Practice, *T88*
Words: *a, I, like, my, see*

⏱ **Oral Language: Vocabulary,** *T89*
Using Action Words

Vocabulary Reader

DAY 2

Daily Routines, *T90–T91*
Calendar, Message, High-Frequency Words

⏱ **Phonemic Awareness** T

Reading the Big Book, *T92–T93*

⏱ **Comprehension Strategy,** *T92*
Predict/Infer

⏱ **Comprehension Skill,** *T92*
Cause and Effect **T**

⏱ **Phonics,** *T94–T95*
Initial Consonant *v* **T**

⏱ **High-Frequency Word,** *T96–T97*
New Word: *to* **T**

⏱ **Word and Picture Book,** *T97*

Leveled Reader

High-Frequency Word Practice, *T98*
Building Sentences

Vocabulary Reader

⏱ **Vocabulary Expansion,** *T99*
Using Action Words

Listening/Speaking/Viewing, *T99*

 Half-Day Kindergarten

Focus on lessons for tested skills marked with **T**. Then choose other activities as time allows.

Target Skills of the Week

Phonemic Awareness	Onset and Rime; Initial Sound /v/; Blending Phonemes
Phonics	Initial Consonant: *Vv*; Words with Short *a*
Comprehension	Cause and Effect; Predict/Infer
Vocabulary	High-Frequency Words; Using Action Words
Fluency	Phonics Library; Word and Picture Book

DAY 3

A Vat
by Elizabeth Kiley
illustrated by Bob Kolar

Daily Routines, *T100–T101*
Calendar, Message, High-Frequency Words

◎ **Phonemic Awareness** **T**

Reading the Big Book, *T102–T107*

◎ **Comprehension Strategy,** *T103*
Predict/Infer

◎ **Comprehension Skill,** *T103*
Cause and Effect **T**

◎ **Concepts of Print,** *T104, T105*
Match Spoken Words to Print **T**

◎ **Phonics,** *T108*
Review Initial Consonant *v*; Blending Short *a* Words **T**

◎ **Reading Decodable Text,** *T109–T111*
"A Vat"

Vocabulary Reader

Leveled Reader

Building Words, *T112*
Words with Short *a*

Shared Writing, *T113*
Writing a Story

DAY 4

Friends Help Friends

Daily Routines, *T114–T115*
Calendar, Message, High-Frequency Words

◎ **Phonemic Awareness** **T**

Reading the Social Studies Link,
T116–T117

◎ **Comprehension Strategy,** *T116*
Predict/Infer

Comprehension Skill, *T116*
Cause and Effect **T**

◎ **Concepts of Print,** *T117*
Match Spoken Words to Print **T**

◎ **Phonics,** *T118–T119*
Blending Short *a* Words **T**

Vocabulary Reader

Leveled Reader

Building Words, *T120*
Words with Short *a*

Interactive Writing, *T121*
Writing Sentences

DAY 5

Daily Routines, *T122–T123*
Calendar, Message, High-Frequency Words

◎ **Phonemic Awareness** **T**

Revisiting the Literature, *T124*

◎ **Comprehension Skill,** *T124*
Cause and Effect **T**

◎ **Building Fluency,** *T125*

◎ **Phonics Review,** *T126*
Consonants, Short *a* Words **T**

High-Frequency Word Review, *T127*
Words: *I, see, my, like, a, to* **T**

◎ **Word and Picture Book,** *T127*

Vocabulary Reader

Leveled Reader

Building Words, *T128*
Words with Short *a*

Independent Writing, *T129*
Journals: Recording Information

Concepts of Print lessons teach important foundational skills for Phonics.

Managing Flexible Groups

DAY 1

WHOLE CLASS

- Daily Routines (TE pp. T80–T81)
- Teacher Read Aloud: *The Lion and the Mouse* (TE pp. T82–T85)
- Phonemic Awareness lesson (TE pp. T86–T87)

SMALL GROUPS

Organize small groups according to children's needs.

TEACHER-LED GROUPS
- Begin Practice Book pp. 139, 140, 141, 142. (TE pp. T83, T87)
- Introduce Phonics Center. (TE p. T87)
- Leveled Reader

INDEPENDENT GROUPS
- Complete Practice Book pp. 139, 140, 141, 142. (TE pp. T83, T87)
- Use Phonics Center. (TE p. T87)

English Language Learners Support is provided in the Reaching All Learners notes throughout the week.

DAY 2

WHOLE CLASS

- Daily Routines (TE pp. T90–T91)
- Big Book: *My Dad and I* (TE pp. T92–T93)
- Phonics lesson (TE pp. T94–T95)
- High-Frequency Word lesson (TE pp. T96–T97)

TEACHER-LED GROUPS
- Begin Practice Book pp. 143, 144. (TE pp. T95, T97)
- Write letters *V, v*; begin handwriting Blackline Master 170 or 204. (TE p. T95)
- Introduce Phonics Center. (TE p. T95)
- Leveled Reader
- Vocabulary Reader

INDEPENDENT GROUPS
- Complete Practice Book pp. 143, 144. (TE pp. T95, T97)
- Complete Blackline Master 170 or 204.
- Use Phonics Center. (TE p. T95)
- **Fluency Practice** Reread Word and Picture Book: *I Like*  . (Practice Book pp. 219–220)

Independent Activities

- Complete Practice Book pages 139–148.
- Complete penmanship practice (Teacher's Resouce Blackline Masters 170 or 204 and 157 or 183).
- Reread familiar Phonics Library or Word and Picture Book stories.
- Share trade books from Leveled Bibliography. (See pp. T4–T5)

DAY 3

- Daily Routines (TE pp. T100–T101)
- Big Book: *My Dad and I* (TE pp. T102–T107)
- Phonics lesson (TE p. T108)

TEACHER-LED GROUPS

- Begin Practice Book pp. 145, 146. (TE pp. T106, T108)
- Write letters *A, a;* begin handwriting Blackline Master 157 or 183.
- Read Phonics Library: "A Vat." (TE pp. T109–T111)
- Leveled Reader
- Vocabulary Reader

INDEPENDENT GROUPS

- Complete Practice Book pp. 145, 146. (TE pp. T106, T108)
- Complete Blackline Master 157 or 183.
- **Fluency Practice** Reread Phonics Library: "A Vat." (TE pp. T109–T111)

DAY 4

- Daily Routines (TE pp. T114–T115)
- Social Studies Link: *Friends Help Friends* (TE pp. T116–T117)
- Phonics lesson (TE pp. T118–T119)

TEACHER-LED GROUPS

- Begin Practice Book p. 147. (TE p. T119)
- Introduce the Phonics Center. (TE p. T119)
- **Fluency Practice** Reread Word and Picture Book: *I Like* 🎂 .
- Leveled Reader
- Vocabulary Reader

INDEPENDENT GROUPS

- Complete Practice Book p. 147. (TE p. T119)
- **Fluency Practice** Color and reread Phonics Library: "A Vat." (TE pp. T109–T111)
- Use Phonics Center. (TE p. T119)

DAY 5

- Daily Routines (TE pp. T122–T123)
- Rereading (TE pp. T124–T125)
- Phonics and High-Frequency Word Review (TE pp. T126–T127)

TEACHER-LED GROUPS

- Begin Blackline Master 36 (TE p. T125)
- Read Word and Picture Book: *I Like My* 🏫 .
- Begin Practice Book p. 148. (TE p. T127)
- **Fluency Practice** Reread the Take-Home version of "A Vat."
- Leveled Reader
- Vocabulary Reader

INDEPENDENT GROUPS

- Complete Blackline Master 36 (TE p. T125)
- Complete Practice Book p. 148. (TE p. T127)
- **Fluency Practice** Reread Word and Picture Book: *I Like My* 🏫 . Reread a favorite Phonics Library or Leveled Reader story.

- Retell or reread Little Big Books.
- Listen to Big Book Audio CDs.
- Use the Phonics Center and other Centers. (See pp. T78–T79)

Turn the page for more independent activities.

Independent Activities

Assign these activities at any time during the week while you work with small groups.

Differentiated Instruction

- **Handbook for English Language Learners** pp. 124–133

- **Extra Support Handbook** pp. 120–129

Additional Independent Activities

- **Classroom Management Handbook**, pp. 82–89

- **Challenge Handbook**, pp. 28–29

Look for more activities in the **Classroom Management Kit.**

Setting Up Centers

ABC Phonics Center

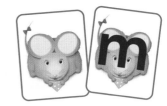

| **Materials** | Phonics Center materials for Theme 4, Week 2 |

Children continue to work with letters and letter sounds this week. They also build words with the letters *v, h, m, t,* and short *a.* Prepare materials for the Days 1, 2, and 4 activities. Cut apart the letter/picture grids and bag them in plastic according to color. Put out the Workmats and open the Direction Chart to the appropriate day. Follow the **Phonics Center** Routine. See pages T87, T95, and T119 for this week's **Phonics Center** activities.

Book Center

| **Materials** | books about friends • class books |

Children continue to explore books about friends. You might also feature class-made books in the Book Center. Children like to read and reread their own work. Consider making "library cards" to attach to these books. Children can sign their names on the cards to show that they've read them. See page T83 for this week's Book Center activity.

Best Friends
by Mrs. Lee's Class

Kevin
Sara

Writing Center

Materials crayons • markers • lined and unlined paper • old magazines • scissors ....

Children make a collage of action photographs and label the pictures with verbs. As needed, help children to cut out small pictures. Later, children draw and label pictures showing activities they do with their friends and family. They begin a *Best Friends* book based on the Shared Writing activity, page T121. See pages T89, T107, and T121 for this week's Writing Center activities.

Art Center

Materials construction paper • crayons or paints ....

Children draw illustrations for a *Best Friends* book. You can bind the Class Book, using yarn, paper fasteners, or heavy-duty staples. If possible, laminate the pages first to anticipate the wear and tear of many rereadings. See pages T93 and T99 for this week's Art Center activities.

DAY 1
week 2

Day at a Glance
T80–T89

Learning to Read
Teacher Read Aloud, *T82*
Phonemic Awareness: */v/, T86*

Word Work
High-Frequency Word Practice, *T88*

Writing & Oral Language
Oral Language, *T89*

Daily Routines

Calendar

Reading the Calendar Point to and read the day and date on the calendar. Point out that this is the first day of the school week. Have children find the first day of the month and practice using the word *first* in oral sentences.

Sunday	Monday	Tuesday	Wednesday	Thursday	Friday	Saturday
			1	2	3	4
5	6	7	8	9	10	11
12	13	14	15	16	17	18
19	20	21	22	23	24	25
26	27	28	29	30	31	

Daily Message

Modeled Writing
Use the word *first* in today's message.

> Today is the <u>first</u> day of our school week.

Word Wall

High-Frequency Words Today, children can take turns finding words with a pointer as you call them out.

I	a	see	my

Word Cards for these words appear on pages R8–R9.

Daily Phonemic Awareness

Blending and Segmenting Onset and Rime

- Play a word sounds game. I'll say some sounds. You put the sounds together to make a word: /s/ /ay/ (say); /l/ /et/ (let); /n/ /ose/ (nose).

- Now I will say a word. You raise your hand when you can tell me the beginning sound and the rest of the word.

Blending Phonemes

- This time I'll say all the separate sounds in a word. You put them together to make the word: /p/ /ĭ/ /g/ (pig); /h/ /ŏ/ /g/ (hog); /h/ /ō/ /m/ (home).

- Continue the game with other words with two or three sounds.

- For children who need help, try using familiar names: /m/ /ī/ /k/ (Mike).

To help children plan their day, tell them that they will–

- listen to a story called *The Lion and the Mouse.*

- meet a new Alphafriend.

- label pictures with action words in the Writing Center.

Read Aloud

OBJECTIVES

- Develop oral language (listening, responding).
- Preview comprehension skill.

READ ALOUD

WEEK 2

Selection Summary

A mighty lion spares the life of a tiny mouse. The mouse returns the favor by gnawing through the rope in which the lion was trapped.

Key Concept A little friend can be a great friend.

English Language Learners

Introduce new vocabulary as needed. Pause to ask yes/no questions to check comprehension. Also encourage children to repeat parts of the lion's and the mouse's lines.

INSTRUCTION

Teacher Read Aloud

Building Background

Read the title aloud. Talk about lions and mice. Do children think a little mouse could (or would) help a great, strong lion?

Point out that a fable is a story in which animals talk and act as people do. Fables teach lessons that people can learn, too.

COMPREHENSION STRATEGY
Predict/Infer

Teacher Modeling Remind children how important it is to predict what a story is about before reading. Model the strategy.

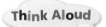 **Think Aloud** When I read the title of the story, "The Lion and the Mouse," I can predict what the story will be about. It will be about a lion and a mouse. Look at the picture with me. I see a lion and a mouse. But I think they're make-believe because animals don't talk to each other. You listen and see if that's right.

COMPREHENSION SKILL
Cause and Effect

Teacher Modeling Explain that it's also helpful to think about why things happen the way they do in a story. Model the strategy.

Think Aloud I want to know why this lion is talking to this mouse. I'll read to find out.

Listening to the Story

Hold your Teacher's Edition so that children can see page T85 as you read. Note that the art is also available on the back of the Theme Poster.

Help make this traditional fable come alive for children by using a deep, gruff voice for the lion and a high, squeaky voice for the mouse.

Responding

Oral Language: Retelling the Story Model how to confirm your predictions by reminding children that you thought the story would be about a make-believe lion and a mouse. Then help them retell parts of the story.

Would a lion and a mouse be friends in real life?

What caused the lion to wake up from his nap?

Why did the lion laugh when the mouse said she would help?

How did the mouse get the lion out of the net?

What did you learn about friends from the story?

Practice Book Children will complete **Practice Book** pages 139–140 during small group time. Children can use the story props on **Blackline Masters** 67–68 to retell the story.

Book Center

Stock your Book Center with books about friends. Include newer titles as well as classics like *May I Bring a Friend?* by Beatrice Schenk de Regniers, *Best Friends for Frances* by Russell Hoban, *The Very Lonely Firefly* by Eric Carle, *Friend Frog* by Alma Flor Ada, and *A Weekend with Wendell* by Kevin Henkes.

Practice Book page 139

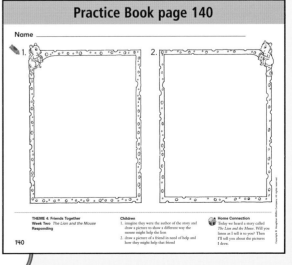

Practice Book page 140

The Lion and the Mouse

A Fable by Aesop

One fine day, a mighty lion was snoozing peacefully when a tiny creature scampered across his nose, tickling his whiskers. Quick as a lightning bolt, the lion trapped the little creature under his great paw.

"What is this? A tiny mouse," the lion said to himself as he peeked under his paw. "How dare you disturb my sleep!" snarled the lion. "Do you know who I am?"

"Oh, yes, Mighty King," squeaked the little mouse, quivering in fear. "I am so sorry. I didn't see you sleeping there."

"Well, now that I'm awake, I think you'd make a tasty snack," said the lion. And with that he began to play with the mouse's long tail, as most cats do with their next meal.

"Oh, please, Mighty King," said the little mouse. "Please let me go." (**Ask:** Do you think the lion will eat the mouse or let her go? Why do you think that? Listen to what happens to find out if you're right.)

"Why should I?" snapped the lion, enjoying this game of cat-and-mouse.

"If you do me this favor and spare my life," replied the mouse, "I promise to help you someday."

Now this made the mighty lion roar with laughter. "How could a tiny creature like you *ever* help me—the mightiest animal in the land?"

"I'm not sure," said the mouse. "But I will be your good friend, and will come to help you whenever you need me. I promise!"

"Well," said the lion, "you did make me laugh. And that's something no one has been able to do for a long time. So I will let you go." And with that, the lion lifted his paw and the little mouse scampered away. (**Ask:** Did you predict what the lion would do with the mouse? Why did the lion let the mouse go?)

A few days later, the lion was snoozing in the tall grass after his noonday meal. Suddenly a huge net fell over him. Hunters! The lion was taken by surprise. He struggled and snarled and tore at the strong rope. But the more he fought, the more tangled he became in the hunters' strong net.

The lion roared a mighty roar. "Someone, please help! Help me out of this net."

But all the animals that could hear him just ran away from his fearsome roar—all except the tiny mouse, that is. (**Ask:** Why did all the animals run away?)

"That's my friend the lion," said the little mouse. "He sounds as if he's in trouble. I must go and see if I can help. (**Ask:** Why did the mouse say this?)

So the mouse ran as fast as her tiny legs would carry her. And when she finally reached him, the lion was so tangled in the hunters' net that he had lost hope of getting away.

The mouse ran to the lion and, looking him straight in the eye, whispered, "Mighty King, I am here to help."

Opening one eye, the lion sighed, "How can you possibly help me? You are so little, and this net is so strong. Not even I—King of the Beasts—can break through it."

"You may be surprised," replied the mouse. And without wasting another breath, she set to work gnawing at the ropes that held the lion. Without stopping for a minute, the mouse chewed through one rope at a time. By afternoon, she had freed the lion's shoulders; and by nightfall, just before the hunters returned, she finished her work, and the mighty lion escaped from the net entirely.

The lion stood and stretched. He shook his great mane. And he lifted the tired little mouse up gently in his paw. "I laughed at you when you said you'd help me," he said. "But I've learned my lesson. It is possible for a very little friend to help a very big friend. Thank you, my small friend."

And then the little mouse ran off. And so did the lion. And the hunters never found him after that.

OBJECTIVES

- Identify pictures whose names begin with /v/.

Materials

- **Alphafriend Cards** *Hattie Horse, Mimi Mouse, Vinny Volcano*
- **Alphafriend CD** Theme 4
- **Alphafolder** *Vinny Volcano*
- **Picture Cards** for *h, m,* and *v*
- **Phonics Center** Theme 4, Week 2, Day 1

Alphafolder *Vinny Volcano*

English Language Learners

The /v/ sound may be difficult for some English language learners to pronounce. In Spanish, for example, /v/ is not distinct from /b/. In other languages, the sound does not occur. Model by exaggerating the differences between the sounds of /v/ and /b/ and /v/ and /f/ in English.

Home Connection

Hand out the take-home version of Vinny Volcano's song. Ask children to share the song with their families. (See **Alphafriends Blackline Masters.**)

PHONEMIC AWARENESS
Beginning Sound

❶ Teach

Introduce the Alphafriend: Vinny Volcano.

Use the Alphafriend routine to introduce Vinny Volcano.

▶ **Alphafriend Riddle** Read these clues:

- This Alphafriend goes va-va-voom when he explodes on top of a mountain. His sound is /v/. Say it with me: /v/.

- He spills lava out of his top. He's very, very scary.

When most hands are up, acknowledge that Vinny is a volcano.

▶ **Pocket Chart** Put Vinny Volcano in a pocket chart. Explain that Vinny's sound is /v/. Say his name, stretching the /v/ sound slightly, and have children echo this.

▶ **Alphafriend CD** Play Vinny Volcano's song. Together, listen for words that start with /v/.

▶ **Alphafolder** Have children look at the illustration and name the /v/ pictures.

▶ **Summarize**

- What is our Alphafriend's name? What is his sound?

- What words in Vinny Volcano's song start with /v/?

- Each time you look at Vinny Volcano, remember the /v/ sound.

Vinny Volcano's Song

(tune: Down in the Valley)

Vinny Volcano is my valentine.

Vinny Volcano, oh won't you be mine?

I'll visit Vinny in the valley below.

I'll bring some violets and a new video.

❷ Guided Practice

Listen for /v/ and compare and review: /h/ and /m/. Put Alphafriends *Hattie Horse* and *Mimi Mouse* opposite *Vinny Volcano* in the pocket chart. Review each character's sound.

Hold up the Picture Cards one at a time. Children signal "thumbs up" for words that start with Vinny Volcano's sound, /v/. When Vinny's pictures are in place, repeat with /h/ and /m/.

Pictures: *van, vase, vet, hand, hat, hen, man, mat, mop*

Tell children they will sort more pictures in the **Phonics Center** today.

❸ Apply

Children complete **Practice Book** pages 141–142 at small group time.

Practice Book page 141

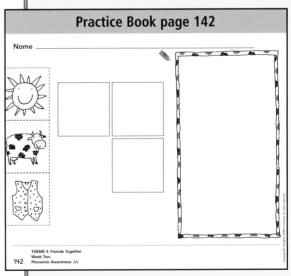

Practice Book page 142

ABC **Phonics** Center

Materials   Phonics Center materials for Theme 4, Week 2, Day 1 ....

Display Day 1 Direction Chart. Children put *Vinny Volcano, Hattie Horse,* and *Mimi Mouse* (without letters) in separate sections of Workmat 3. Then they sort remaining pictures by initial sound: /v/, /h/, and /m/.

OBJECTIVES

- Read high-frequency words.
- Create and write sentences with high-frequency words.

Materials

- **Word Cards** *a, I, like, my, see*
- *Higglety Pigglety: A Book of Rhymes,* page 6
- **Picture Cards** *cat, toys*
- **Punctuation Card** period

High-Frequency Words

Display and read the Word Cards *I, like, see, a,* and *my*.

- Choose a child to read a word and find its match on the Word Wall.

- Remind children that they will see these words often in books. I'll read a poem. Listen for one of these words in it.

- Read "Everybody Says" on page 6 of *Higglety Pigglety*. I heard the word *like* in this poem. Who can find *like* in the poem? Continue, having children match *I* and *my*.

THEME
1

Everybody Says

Everybody says
I look just like my mother.
Everybody says
I'm the image of Aunt Bee.
Everybody says
My nose is like my father's.
But I want to look like ME!

by Dorothy Aldis

6

Higglety Pigglety: A Book of Rhymes, page 6

Have children write sentences.

- Tell children that now that they can read new words, they can write them, too. Start by using **Word Cards** and **Picture Cards** to make sentences.

- Children can write and illustrate one of the sentences or write their own sentences with rebus pictures. They can use temporary phonics spellings for words of their own choosing, but insist on correct spellings of high-frequency words children know.

| I | like | my |  | |

| I | see | my |  | |

TARGET SKILL

ORAL LANGUAGE: VOCABULARY
Using Action Words

❶ Teach

Discuss action words.
- Explain that action words are words that tell what someone or something does.
- Ask children to name some action words they know.

❷ Practice/Apply

Play an action-word game.
- Have some children pantomime actions that you whisper to them. (jump, hug, eat, wave hello, dance)
- Other children name the action words while you record what they say.

Action Words

run	jump
hop	hug
eat	dance

✎ Writing Center

Materials old magazines • drawing paper • crayons

Provide children with old magazines they can look through to find "pictures" of action words. Children can cut and paste the pictures to make a collage. Put the chart from above in the Writing Center to help them label their pictures with action words.

run jump read

Oral Language   **T89**

Day at a Glance
T90–T99

Learning to Read

Big Book, *T92*

Phonics: Initial Consonant *v, T94*

High-Frequency Word: *to, T96*

Word Work

High-Frequency Word Practice, *T98*

Writing & Oral Language

Vocabulary Expansion, *T99*

Daily Routines

Sunday	Monday	Tuesday	Wednesday	Thursday	Friday	Saturday
			1	2	3	4
5	6	7	8	9	10	11
12	13	14	15	16	17	18
19	20	21	22	23	24	25
26	27	28	29	30	31	

Calendar

Read the Calendar In your calendar routine, introduce ordinal numbers. Say, *Yesterday was the* first *day of the school week and today is the* second *day.* Have children hold up one finger for *first* and two fingers for *second.* Listen for children to use the words *first* and *second* in their conversations.

Daily Message

Modeled Writing
Try to use the words *first* and *second* in your daily message.

Petey got his
first puppy.
His name is Lars.

Word Wall

High-Frequency Words Play "Pass the Pointer." Have children take turns finding Word Wall words with a pointer as you call them out.

I	see	a	like

Word Cards for these words appear on pages R8–R9.

Daily Phonemic Awareness

Blending and Segmenting Onset and Rime

- Display the **Picture Cards** *hen, hat,* and *van*.

- I'll say some sounds. You put them together to name a picture. Listen: /v//an/. What word is that? That's right, *van*.

- Now choose a **Picture Card** and ask children to say the beginning sound and the rest of the word.

- Continue with the names for the other pictures.

Blending Phonemes

- This time I'll say some separate sounds. You put them together to make an action word: /r//ŭ//n/. (run) Now here's a hard one, with four sounds. Listen: /j//ŭ//m//p/. (jump)

- Continue with other action words with two to four sounds.

Getting Ready to Learn

To help children plan their day, tell them that they will–

- listen to a **Big Book:** *My Dad and I.*

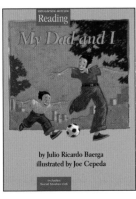

- learn the new letters *V* and *v,* and see words that begin with *v.*

- draw pictures in the Art Center.

OBJECTIVES

- Introduce concepts of print.
- Develop story language.
- Reinforce comprehension strategy and comprehension skill.

My Dad and I

Selection Summary Through a series of shared activities—playing soccer, drawing, singing—Rafa and his dad show how they are very best friends.

Key Concept Dads are friends, too.

Reading the Big Book

Building Background

Ask children what sorts of fun things they do with their dads, moms, or other favorite people. Then tell children they'll hear a story called *My Dad and I*. The story tells about a boy and his dad and the things they like to do together.

COMPREHENSION STRATEGY
Predict/Infer

Teacher Modeling Model the strategy as you page through the book.

 **Think Aloud** Before I start to read, I want to know a little about the story. I can tell from the title and the picture on the cover that this book is about a boy and his dad. What will they do? I see they play soccer together. What else might they do? Maybe they'll go to the movies. Let's see if I'm right. You listen as I read.

COMPREHENSION SKILL
Cause and Effect

Teacher Modeling Tell children that good readers and listeners are also curious about *why* things happen in a story.

Think Aloud As I read, let's stop every once in a while to think about what happens in the story and why it happens.

Big Book Read Aloud

As you read, pause briefly to invite children to chime in on the repeated line: *We are very best friends.* Track the print with a pointer indicating a voice-to-print match.

Responding

Oral Language: Personal Response Encourage children to express their feelings about the story.

- What did you like about the story? Why?
- What did Rafa and his dad do together?
- How do you know that Rafa and his dad are best friends?
- What do you do with your best friend?

Art Center

Materials drawing paper • crayons and markers

In the Art Center, have children draw pictures of things they do with their best friends. Save these pictures for the action words activity on T99. Then bind the pages together to make a "My Best Friends" class book.

 English Language Learners

List activities that learners might do with family members, such as: play ball, ride bicycles, read books, go shopping. Ask: *Who plays ball with _____? Who goes shopping with _____?* Record children's names by the appropriate activities. Preview the illustrations to identify the activities Rafa does with his dad.

 Extra Support/ Intervention

To help children summarize the story, have them look at individual illustrations and describe what they see. Encourage the use of words such as *first, then,* and *in the beginning of the book.*

OBJECTIVES

- Identify words that begin with /v/.
- Identify pictures whose names begin with /v/.
- Form the letters *V, v.*

Materials

- **Alphafriend Cards** *Hattie Horse, Mimi Mouse, Vinny Volcano*
- **Letter Cards** *h, m, v*
- **Picture Cards** for *h, m, v*
- **Blackline Master** 170
- **Phonics Center** Theme 4, Week 2, Day 2

Vinnie Volcano's Song

(tune: Down in the Valley)

Vinnie Volcano is my valentine.

Vinnie Volcano, oh won't you be mine?

I'll visit Vinny in the valley below.

I'll bring some violets and a new video.

Extra Support/ Intervention

To help children remember the sound for *v*, point out that the letter's name gives a clue to the sound: *v, /v/.*

INSTRUCTION

PHONICS
Initial Consonant *v*

❶ Phonemic Awareness Warm-Up

Beginning Sound Demonstrate how to make a "V" for "victory" sign with your fingers. Then sing or read the lyrics of Vinny Volcano's song, and have children echo you line-for-line. Have them listen for the /v/ words and make the "victory sign" for each one they hear. See Theme Resources page R3 for music and lyrics.

❷ Teach Phonics

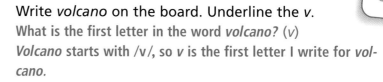

Beginning Letter Hold up the *Vinny Volcano* card with his letter. The letter *v* stands for the sound /v/, as in *volcano.* When you see a *v*, remember *Vinny Volcano.* That will help you remember the sound /v/.

Write *volcano* on the board. Underline the *v*. What is the first letter in the word *volcano?* (*v*) *Volcano* starts with /v/, so *v* is the first letter I write for *vol-cano.*

❸ Guided Practice

Compare and Review: *v, h, m* In a pocket chart, display the **Letter Cards** as shown and the **Picture Cards** in random order. Review the sounds for *v, h,* and *m.* In turn, children can name a picture, say the beginning sound, and put the card below the right letter. Tell children that they will sort more pictures in the

Penmanship Rhyme: V

Start at the top
Slant in just a little.
Back up to the top.
Then meet in the middle.

Penmanship Rhyme: v

Little v's lines
Still meet in the middle.
It's just like the capital,
Only it's little.

Penmanship: Writing V, v Tell children they'll learn to write the letters that stand for /v/: capital *V* and small *v*. Write each letter as you recite the penmanship rhyme. Children can listen to the rhyme as they "write" the letter in the air.

❹ Apply

Have children complete **Practice Book** page 143 at small group time.

For additional penmanship practice, assign **Blackline Master** 170. Penmanship practice for the continuous stroke style is available on **Blackline Master** 204.

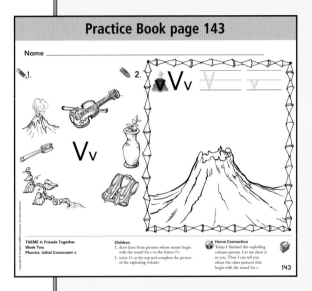

Practice Book page 143

ABC Phonics Center

Materials — Phonics Center materials for Theme 4, Week 2, Day 2 ....

Display Day 2 Direction Chart. Children put *Vinny Volcano, Hattie Horse,* and *Mimi Mouse* (with letters) in separate sections of Workmat 3. Then they sort remaining pictures by initial letter: *v, h,* or *m.*

INSTRUCTION

HIGH-FREQUENCY WORD
New Word: *to*

❶ Teach

Introduce the word *to*. Tell children they'll learn a new word today. It's a word they'll often see in stories and that they use all the time when they speak. Say *to* and use it in context.

We go *to* school.   We like *to* read.   I like *to* play.

- Before writing *to* on the board, ask children what letter they'd expect to see first. Confirm their predictions and write *to*.

- Spell *to* with me: *t-o, to.* Then lead children in a chant, clapping on each beat, to help them remember the spelling: *t-o, to! t-o, to!*

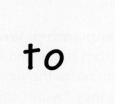

Word Wall Add *to* to the Word Wall, and remind children to look there when they need to spell the word. Briefly review the other words on the board. Celebrate children's growing bank of known words.

❷ Guided Practice

Build these sentences one at a time. Tell children that now they'll read their new word. Display these sentences. Call on specific children to take turns reading. Leave the pocket chart out for children to use as a model for their own sentences.

OBJECTIVES

- Read and write the high-frequency word *to*.

Materials

- **Word Cards** *I, like, to*
- **Picture Cards** *dig, hop, run*
- **Punctuation Card** period
- ***Higglety Pigglety: A Book of Rhymes,*** page 31

TO MARKET, TO MARKET

To market, to market, to buy a fat pig,
Home again, home again, jiggety jig.
To market, to market, to buy a fat hog,
Home again, home again, jiggety jog.
To market, to market, to buy
a plum bun,
Home again, home again,
market is done.

a Mother Goose Rhyme

Higglety Pigglety: A Book of Rhymes,
page 31

Display *Higglety Piggley: A Book of Rhymes,* page 31.

- Read the rhyme "To Market, To Market" aloud.

- Remember I told you that you'd see our new word in books. Who can find the word *To* in the title of this poem?

- Next, read the first line, tracking the print. What do you notice? Help children note that *To* appears with a capital letter at the beginning of a line and with a small *t* the other times.

- Choose children to find and read *to* each time it appears.

❸ Apply

- Have children complete **Practice Book** page 144 at small group time. Children will read and write *to* as they complete the **Practice Book** page.

- Pass out copies of the story on **Practice Book** pages 219–220, *I Like* 🎂. Read the title aloud. Ask children to predict what the mother and children are making.

For each page, have children look at the picture and tell what the boy and girl like to do. Have them read the page silently. Then ask a child to read the page aloud. Use questions such as the following to prompt discussion:

Page 1 What does each child like to do?

Page 2 Did we guess what they were making?

Pages 3–4 Whose birthday is it? What does the family like to do at a party? How do you like to celebrate birthdays?

Then have children count the high-frequency words in the story: How many times can you find the word *I* in this story? the word *like*? the word *to?*

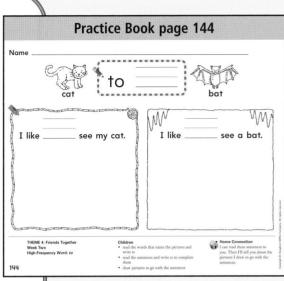

Practice Book page 144

Practice Book pages 219–220

Monitoring Student Progress

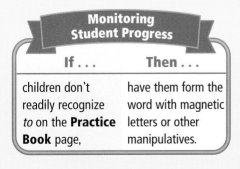

If . . .	Then . . .
children don't readily recognize *to* on the **Practice Book** page,	have them form the word with magnetic letters or other manipulatives.

High-Frequency Word **T97**

OBJECTIVES
• Read high-frequency words.
• Create and write sentences with high-frequency words.

PRACTICE

High-Frequency Words

Build sentences with words and pictures.

• Make a predictable chart with children to practice reading high-frequency words. Start out with your own contribution by telling something you like to do. Write or draw the action.

• Record children's ideas and add their names. Children will want to read the completed chart many times.

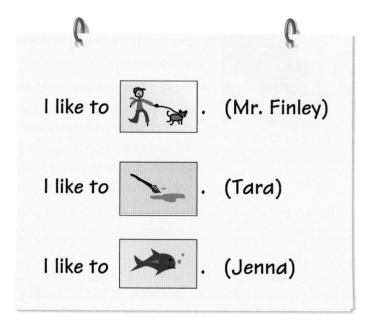

Have children write sentences.

• Have children copy and illustrate their sentences.

VOCABULARY EXPANSION
Using Action Words

Listening/Speaking/Viewing

Discuss action words.

- Remind children that the story *My Dad and I* is about a boy and his dad doing fun things together. Browse through the book, choosing children to describe what they see.

- Remind children that the author uses many action words, or verbs, to tell what Rafa and his dad do together.

- List some of the words from the text.

Actions

play soccer	sing	laugh
play in pool	tell jokes	
dance	draw	

Vocabulary Support

The Vocabulary Reader can be used to develop and reinforce vocabulary related to the instruction for this week.

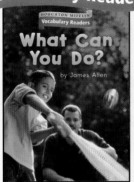

Vocabulary Reader

HOUGHTON MIFFLIN
Vocabulary Readers

What Can You Do?
by James Allen

🎨 Art Center

Materials drawing paper • crayons or paints

Have children look at the "Best Friends" pictures they drew earlier. Have them add another picture showing themselves and a family member doing something together. Remind children of the action words you listed *(sing, swim, draw, dance)* if they want to label their pictures.

DAY 3
week 2

Day at a Glance
T100–T113

Learning to Read

Big Book, *T102*

Phonics: Reviewing Consonant *v*; Blending Short *a* Words, *T108*

Word Work

Building Words, *T112*

Writing & Oral Language

Shared Writing, *T113*

Daily Routines

Sunday	Monday	Tuesday	Wednesday	Thursday	Friday	Saturday
			1	2	3	4
5	6	7	8	9	10	11
12	13	14	15	16	17	18
19	20	21	22	23	24	25
26	27	28	29	30	31	

first   second   third

Calendar

Reading the Calendar Read the day and date, and ask a child to point to it on the calendar. Continue to talk about *first*, *second*, and *third*. Have children hold up one finger for *first*, two fingers for *second*, and three for *third*. Encourage children to use *first*, *second*, and *third* throughout the day.

Daily Message

Modeled Writing Point out the use of action words and the week's high-frequency word in your daily message.

We will go to gym today.

Mr. Chang will teach us how to dance.

Word Wall

High-Frequency Words Choose a child to point to and read the new word that was added to the Word Wall this week, *to*. Have children compare *to* with other words on the Word Wall. For example: *to* has two letters like *an* and *my*; *to* is longer than *I* and *a*, but shorter than *see* and *like*. Continue reading the remaining words.

to	a	my	like

Word Cards for these words appear on pages R8–R9.

⊙ Daily Phonemic Awareness

Blending and Segmenting Onset and Rime

- Play a word sound game. I'll say some sounds. You put them together to make words: /k//an/ (can); /h//iz/ (his).

- Now I'll say a word and you take it apart. Say the beginning sound and then the rest of the word *fur*: (/f//ur/); *bear* (/b//ear/); *most* (/m//ost/).

- Continue with other one-syllable words or names of children.

Blending Phonemes

- Read "Humpty Dumpty" on page 19 of *Higglety Pigglety*.

- Tell children that you will say some separate sounds and they should put them together to make a word from the poem. Say these sounds: /m//ĕ//n/ (men); /g//r//ā//t/ (great).

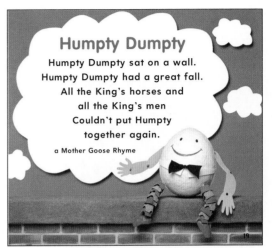

Higglety Pigglety: A Book of Rhymes, page 19

To help children plan their day, tell them that they will—

- reread and talk about the **Big Book** *My Dad and I.*

- read a story called "A Vat."

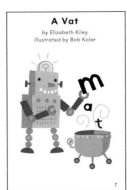

- help write a "My Best Friend" Big Book.

Reading the Big Book

Reading for Understanding

Reread the story, stopping for children to chime in. Pause for Comprehension points.

 English Language Learners

After reading page 8, pause and ask children what their dad, mom, friend, or relative teaches them to do. Have children respond following the model: *[Person's Name] teaches me how to ___.* Check for use of the infinitive in the response.

My name is Rafael.
My dad's name is Rafael.

1

My dad calls me Rafa.
I call him Dad.

2

We are very best friends.

3

2

My dad teaches me
how to play soccer.
I am getting better.

4

We are very best friends.

5

4

I try to teach my dad
how to sing.
He is getting better.

6

We are very best friends.

7

7

My dad teaches me
how to swim.
We like to play in the pool.

8

We are very best friends.

9

9

I try to teach my dad
how to tell new jokes.
We like to laugh.

10

We are very best friends.

11

10   11

COMPREHENSION STRATEGY

Predict/Infer

title page
Teacher-Student Modeling Remind children that predictions may or may not be accurate.

- Before reading, I predicted the boy and his dad might go to the movies, but that didn't happen. Maybe next time my ideas will be the same as the author's.

- What do the title and picture tell us?

CRITICAL THINKING

Guiding Comprehension

pages 4–7

- **NOTING DETAILS/DRAWING CONCLUSIONS** Do Rafa and his dad have fun together? How do you know?

COMPREHENSION SKILL

Cause and Effect

pages 10–11
Teacher-Student Modeling We know it's important to understand why things happen in a story. What made Rafa's dad laugh? (jokes) Let's look for other reasons things happen.

Oral Language

getting better When we work hard to learn something new, we "get better" at it.

CRITICAL THINKING
Guiding Comprehension

page 12

- **DRAWING CONCLUSIONS** How do you know Rafa is just learning how to dance? (He steps on his dad's toes.)

page 13

- **NOTING DETAILS** Is Rafa getting better at dancing? How do you know? (He's not stepping on his dad's toes.)

TARGET SKILL

REVISITING THE TEXT
Concepts of Print

page 12

Word Spacing

Choose a child to point to each word on page 12. **How can we tell where one word stops and the next one begins?** (by the space between them)

My dad teaches me how to dance. Sometimes I step on his toes.
12

We are very best friends.
13

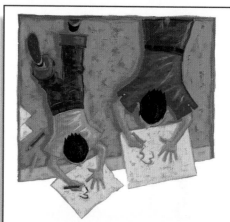

I try to teach my dad how to draw. We make each other laugh.
14

We are very best friends.
15

I love my dad.
16

My dad loves me.
17

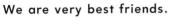
We are very best friends.

18

8

19

TARGET SKILL

REVISITING THE TEXT

Concepts of Print

pages 1–18

Matching Spoken Words to Print

To emphasize speech-to-print match, use the repetitive sentence *We are very best friends.* Read the sentence aloud several times and choose children to point to each word.

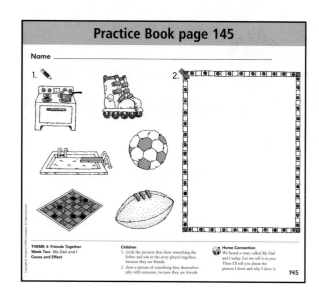

Practice Book page 145

Name _____

1. ✏️

2.

Children
1. circle the pictures that show something the father and son in the story played together, because they are friends
2. draw a picture of something they themselves play with someone, because they are friends

🎲 **Home Connection**
We heard a story called *My Dad and I* today. Let me tell it to you. Then I'll tell you about the picture I drew and why I drew it.

145

Responding

Oral Language: Retelling

Use these prompts to help children summarize *My Dad and I*.

- **What did you like about this story? Tell us in your own words.**
- **Who remembers what Rafa and his dad liked to do together?** (play soccer, sing, swim, tell jokes, dance, draw)
- **Why do you think Rafa said he and his dad are best friends?** (They like to do things together; they love each other very much.)
- **What picture did you like the best? Why?**

Practice Book Children will complete **Practice Book** page 145 during small group time.

Challenge

Have partners think of another episode to add to this story. They can draw what happens and then share it with the group.

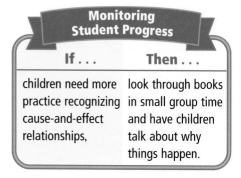

Monitoring Student Progress

If . . .	Then . . .
children need more practice recognizing cause-and-effect relationships,	look through books in small group time and have children talk about why things happen.

 Writing Center

Point out that family members are also friends. Ask children to think of ways family members help each other. Children can draw pictures of family members helping each other. They can label their pictures *My _____ and I*. Some might even want to try completing the sentences with words of their own. They can use temporary phonics spellings to do so.

OBJECTIVES

- Identify words with initial consonant *v*, /v/.
- Blend and read words with *b, h, m, n, r, s, t, v*, and short *a*.

Materials

- **Alphafriend CD** Theme 4
- **Alphafriend Cards** *Andy Apple, Tiggy Tiger, Vinny Volcano*
- **Letter Cards** *a, b, h, m, n, r, s, t, v*
- **Blending Routines Card 1**

Practice Book page 146

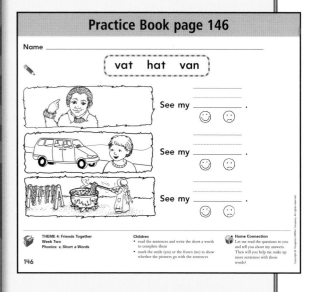

Monitoring Student Progress

If . . .	Then . . .
children have trouble blending words such as *bat, sat,* and *ham,*	repeat this lesson using **Blending Routines Card 2,** *Sound-by-Sound Blending.*

INSTRUCTION

PHONICS
Blending Short *a* Words

❶ Teach: Connect Sounds to Letters

Review consonant *v*. Ask children which letter and sound they think of when they see Vinny Volcano.

- Play Vinny Volcano's song, and have children make the victory sign for each /v/ word.
- Write *V* and *v* on the board, and list *v* words from the song.

Introduce short *a*. Tell children they'll build a word with *v*, but first they'll need a vowel ("helper letter").

- Display *Andy Apple*. You remember Andy Apple. Andy's letter is the vowel *a*, and the sound *a* usually stands for is /ă/. Say /ă/ with me.

Model Blending Routine 1. Now show the **Letter Cards** *a* and *t*. Have children identify each letter and the sound it stands for.

- Review blending the sounds as you point to each letter with a sweeping motion. I say the sounds in order: first /ă/, then /t/. I hold each sound until I say the next one, *ăăăt, at*. I've made the word *at*. Repeat, having children blend and pronounce *at* with you.
- Show **Letter Cards** *v, a,* and *t*. Model blending the sounds as you point to the letters with a sweeping motion: *vvvăăăt, vat*. Repeat, having children blend the word on their own.
- Repeat this procedure with *Nat*. Then display *bat, sat,* and *rat,* and have children blend the sounds as you point to the letters.

❷ Guided Practice

Check Understanding. Display the word *hat* and ask individuals to blend the word. Display *mat, rat,* and *van* and have children blend the words, modeling blending as needed. Remind children to hold each sound until they say the next one, *mmmăăăt*. Continue as children blend these words: *ham, tab, sat*. Display the sentence *I see a rat*. Children should recognize the underlined words from the Word Wall. Tell them to blend the other word to read the sentence.

❸ Apply

Children complete **Practice Book** 146 at small group time.

A Vat
by Elizabeth Kiley
illustrated by Bob Kolar

7

Friends Together

PHONICS LIBRARY
Reading Decodable Text
Phonics/Decoding Strategy

Teacher-Student Modeling Discuss using the Phonics/Decoding strategy to read words in the story.

Have children look at the picture on the title page. Tell children that the robot is putting a letter into a vat. Explain that a vat is a pot for holding things.

Think Aloud Let's read the title. I know the first word is *A*. The next word begins with *V*. The sound for *V* is /v/. The other letters are *a* and *t*. I blend the letters to read this word: *vvvăăăt, vat.*

Preview the pictures on pages 8–9. Explain that the robot from the title page is also on these pages. What do you think the robot is making in the vat?

OBJECTIVES

- Apply the phonics skills to decode short *a* words.
- Apply high-frequency words.
- Reread for fluency practice.

mat

8

hat

9

Prompts for Decoding

Have children read each page silently before reading aloud to you. Prompts:

page 8 Write the word *mat* on the board. Model blending the sounds: *mmmăăăt, mat*.

page 9 What will come out of the vat next? How do you know?

page 11 How many rhyming words do you see on this page? What letters are the same in these words?

Word Key

Decodable words with short *a* ———

High-Frequency Words ———

rat

10

mat
hat
rat

11

Oral Language

Discuss the story. Remind children to speak in complete sentences.

- Look at the pictures. What did the robot make? (mats, hats, toy rats)

- What is the robot holding? (letters and signs)

- Where did the robot put all the boxes? (in his truck)

- What do you think he did then? (drove his truck to the toy store)

Identify rhyming words. Ask children to reread the story and identify rhyming words. *(vat, mat, hat, rat)* Then ask children to model blending the words. Remind them to hold each sound until they say the next one. Then have children name other things that the robot could make that would also rhyme with these words.

Build Fluency

Model fluent reading.

- Read aloud page 11. Then have children read the page aloud.

- Have children reread the same page several times until each child can read it aloud smoothly.

Home Connection

Have children color the picture in the take-home version of "A Vat." After rereading on Day 4, they can take it home to read to family members. (See **Phonics Library Blackline Masters.**)

Reading Decodable Text **T111**

PRACTICE

BUILDING WORDS
Words with Short *a*

Model building the word *at*.

- Display the **Letter Cards** *a, b, h, m, N, r, s, t, v*.

- First, I'll stretch out the sounds: *ăăăt*. How many sounds do you hear? The first sound is /ă/. I'll put up *a* in the chart to spell that sound. The next sound is /t/. What letter stands for /t/? Put the **Letter Card** *t* in the chart. Blend /ă/ and /t/ and read *at*.

Model building words that rhyme with *at*.

- Now let's write *vat, vvăăăt*. How many sounds do you hear? The first sound is /v/. What letter stands for /v/? Put the **Letter Card** *v* in the chart. The next sound is /ă/. What letter should I use? Continue with the final sound in *vat*.

- Repeat the procedure to write *hat*. Continue building the following words: *bat, mat, Nat, sat,* and *rat*.

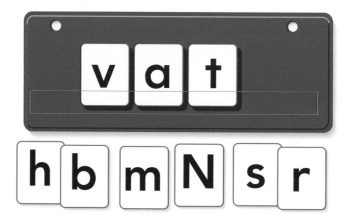

Word Wall Have a child find *at* on the Word Wall. Remind children that they can use *at* to help them read and write words that rhyme with *at*.

Check Understanding Small groups can work together using sandpaper letters or other manipulatives in your collection to make words with short *a*. Ask children to build the word *hat*. Provide corrections as needed. Have children blend and read other words they build.

Extend Practice Ask children to build the words: *van, sat, bat, ham, Sam, man*. Guide them to use the above procedure even though not all of the words rhyme with *at*. Display this sentence: *I like to bat*. Tell children to read the underlined words (from the Word Wall) and to blend the other word to read the sentence.

SHARED WRITING
Writing a Story

- Use action words.
- Participate in a shared writing activity.

- **Big Book** *My Dad and I*
- children's "Best Friend" pictures

Write a story together.
- Have children show each other the "Best Friend" pictures they drew.
- Encourage the group to use action words to describe their drawings. Record their responses.

Read the Shared Writing piece aloud.
- As you read, reinforce the concept of letter, word, and sentence.
- Ask questions such as, Who will point to the word *to?* Where does this sentence start? What mark did we put at the end? Why? How many words are in this sentence? Let's count the words.

We Are Very Best Friends

Maria likes to cook with her mom.
They are very best friends.

David plants a garden with Grandpa Joe.
They are very best friends.

Pedro plays soccer with his dad.
They are very best friends.

Mai likes to sing songs with her sister.
They are very best friends.

DAY 4
week 2

Day at a Glance
T114–T121

Learning to Read
Big Book, *T116*
Phonics: Reviewing Consonant *v;* Blending Short *a* Words, *T118*

Word Work
Building Words, *T120*

Writing & Oral Language
Interactive Writing, *T121*

Daily Routines

Calendar

Reading the Calendar Have children tell you that this is the fourth day of the week. Then ask what day tomorrow will be. Continue to use the words *first, second, third,* and *fourth* during the day.

Sunday	Monday	Tuesday	Wednesday	Thursday	Friday	Saturday
			1	2	3	4
5	6	7	8	9	10	11
12	13	14	15	16	17	18
19	20	21	22	23	24	25
26	27	28	29	30	31	

first second third fourth

Daily Message

Modeled Writing
Use ordinal numbers in your daily message.

We saw the squirrel for the fourth time today. He likes nuts.

Word Wall

High-Frequency Words Hold up cards for Word Wall words. Choose a child to match each card on the board. After the match is made, others chant the spelling of the word: *s-e-e* spells *see; a-n* spells *an.*

see	an	like	my

Word Cards for these words appear on pages R8–R9.

Daily Phonemic Awareness

Blending and Segmenting Onset and Rime

Play "Pat, Pat, Clap." Pat and clap with children as you say: /k//it/, *kit;* /v//an/, *van.*

- Continue with other words from the list. You give the sounds; children supply the whole word on the clap beat.
- Now I'll say a word. You "pat, pat" the beginning and ending sounds, then we'll all clap and say the word again. Listen: *sun.* (/s//un/, *sun*)
- Continue with other words from the list.

Blending Phonemes

- Play a different game this time. Listen as I say some separate sounds. You blend the sounds to make words we use to tell where. Listen: /ŏ//n/ (on). That's right, *on.* Say it with me: /ŏ//n/, *on.*
- Continue with other one-syllable position words.

"Pat, Pat, Clap"

mat	pig	hen
bug	hat	sit
fan	mop	get
lap	jet	run

Getting Ready to Learn

To help children plan their day, tell them that they will—

- read the Social Studies Link: *Friends Help Friends.*

- build new words in the **Phonics Center.**

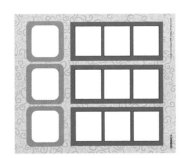

- reread a story called "A Vat."

A Vat
by Elizabeth Kiley
illustrated by Bob Kolar

- Tell why things happen.
- Match spoken words to print.

Big Book

Social Studies Link

Friends Help Friends

HOUGHTON MIFFLIN
Reading

My Dad and I

by Julio Ricardo Baerga
illustrated by Joe Cepeda

Includes:
Social Studies Link

Oral Language

firehouse: A firehouse is a place where fire trucks are kept. Sometimes firefighters even sleep there.

 English Language Learners

Introduce the concept of, and vocabulary for, community helpers with pictures representing the different professions. Play "Who Is It?" Name a profession. Have children find the picture and tell what the person does.

READING THE BIG BOOK
Social Studies Link

Building Background

When you go to the library to find a special book, who helps you find it? Who helps you get your lunch in the cafeteria? Explain that people who help us, such as librarians and cafeteria workers, are our friends. This article tells about some friends who help us. It's called "Friends Help Friends."

Reading for Understanding As you share the selection, invite children's comments.

 COMPREHENSION STRATEGY
Predict/Infer

page 22
Student Modeling Say that each page tells about a helpful friend. Preview the photographs. Ask: Who helps at school? Then browse through more pages to predict other helpers children will hear about.

 COMPREHENSION SKILL
Cause and Effect

Student Modeling Why is the girl working with her teacher? (because teachers help children learn)

**Friends
Help Friends**

Social Studies
Link

21

Friends help friends.
Who helps at school?

22

21

22

Friends help friends.
Who helps at the library?

23

Friends help friends.
Who helps at the park?

24

23

24

Friends help friends.
Who helps at the firehouse?

25

Where do you like to go?
Who are your friends?

26

25

26

CRITICAL THINKING

Guiding Comprehension

page 26

- **MAKING JUDGMENTS** Why are the jobs done by these people important?

TARGET SKILL

REVISITING THE TEXT

Concepts of Print

pages 22–25

Match Spoken Words to Print

- To emphasize speech-to-print match, use the repetitive sentence *Friends help friends.* Read the sentence aloud several times and choose children to point to each word.

Responding

Ask: Do you have friends who help you? Are they teachers, librarians, or police officers? Tell how they have helped you.

REACHING ALL LEARNERS

Challenge

Ask those children who are able to go beyond the story to name other community helpers. They can draw, label, or write about these helpers, following the pattern of the book.

PRACTICE

OBJECTIVES

- Identify initial *v* for words that begin with /v/.
- Blend and read words with consonants and short *a*.

Materials

- *From Apples to Zebras: A Book of ABC's,* pages 9, 14, 23
- **Alphafriend Card** *Andy Apple*
- **Letter Cards** *a, b, h, m, n, r, s, t, v*
- **Picture Cards** *bat, hat, mat*
- **Phonics Center** Theme 4, Week 2, Day 4
- **Blending Routines Card 1**

PHONICS
Blending Short *a* Words

Review consonants *v, h,* and *m*. Cover the labels on page 23 of *From Apples to Zebras.*

- Have children name the pictures together.
- Ask them to predict what letter each word begins with. Uncover the words so that children can check their predictions.
- Repeat the activity to review *h* and *m*.

From Apples to Zebras: A Book of ABC's, page 23

Review short *a*. Remind children that to build words with *v,* they also need a vowel ("helper letter") because every word has at least one of those.

- Ask which Alphafriend stands for the vowel sound /ă/. *(Andy Apple)*
- Display Andy and have children think of other words that start with /ă/. *(ask, answer)*

Review Blending Routine 1. Hold up **Letter Cards** *a* and *t*. Watch and listen as I build a word from the Word Wall: /ă/ /t/, ăăăt, at.

- Put the **Letter Card** *v* in front of *at.* Now let's blend my new word: /v/ /ă/ /t/, vvvăăăt, vat.
- Continue, choosing children to build and blend *hat, mat, bat, rat,* and *sat.*

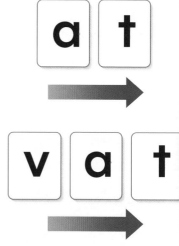

Check Understanding Display the word *hat* and ask individuals to blend the word. For practice with a mix of CVC words, display *mat, sat,* and *Sam* and have children blend the words. Model blending as needed. Remind children to hold each sound until they say the next one. Continue as children blend the following: *bat, man, van.* Display the sentence *I see a vat.* Children should recognize the underlined words from the Word Wall. Tell them to blend the other word to read the sentence.

Home Connection

Challenge children to talk at home about names that begin with *v. (Vincenza, Vera, Victor, Vincent)* See how many names children and their families can list.

Practice/Apply In a pocket chart, display the **Picture Card** *hat*.

Have children say *hat* slowly.

Choose a child to build *hat* in the pocket chart.

Build the words *mat* and *bat*. Ask everyone to read the words aloud.

Have children complete **Practice Book** page 147 at small group time.

In groups today, children will read short *a* words as they reread the **Phonics Library** story "A Vat." See suggestions, pages T109–T111.

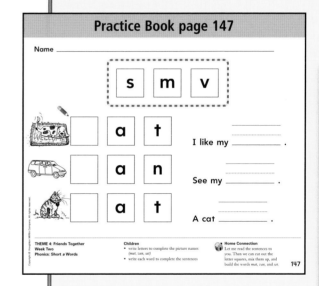

Practice Book page 147

Name _____

| s | m | v |

| | a | t | I like my _____ .

| | a | n | See my _____ .

| | a | t | A cat _____ .

THEME 4: Friends Together
Week Two
Phonics: Short *a* Words

Children
• write letters to complete the picture names (*mat, van, sat*)
• write each word to complete the sentences

Home Connection
Let me read the sentences to you. Then we can cut out the letter squares, mix them up, and build the words *mat, van,* and *sat*.

147

ABC Phonics Center

Materials Phonics Center materials for Theme 4, Week 2, Day 4 ·

Display Day 4 Direction Chart and Workmat 4. Children place a **Picture Card** (*mat, vat,* or *hat*) in the first box and then build the word with **Letter Cards,** sound by sound. In the same way, they build the other short *a* words.

Monitoring Student Progress

If . . .	Then . . .
children don't readily recognize short *a* words,	write the words on cards with short *a* in a second color.

Phonics T119

OBJECTIVES

- Blend consonants with short *a* to read words.

Materials

- Letter Cards *a, b, h, m, N, r, s, t, v*

BUILDING WORDS
Words with Short *a*

Model building the word *vat*.

- Display **Letter Cards** *a, b, h, m, N, s, t,* and *v*.

- Review how to build words. **Let's build *vat*. How many sounds do you hear? The first sound is /v/. I'll put up a *v* to spell that. The next sound is /ă/. What letter stands for that sound? I'll add the letter *a* to the chart. What is the last sound you hear?** Add the letter *t* to the chart.

- Model blending the word, *vvvăăăt, vat*.

- Choose children to build more short *a* words using *b, h, m, N, r,* and *s*.

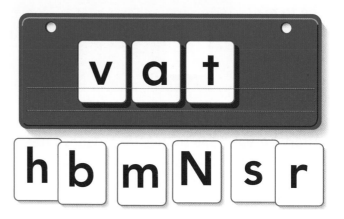

Check Understanding Have groups write short *a* words such as *Nat* on white boards. Provide corrections as needed. They can read their lists of words to a partner.

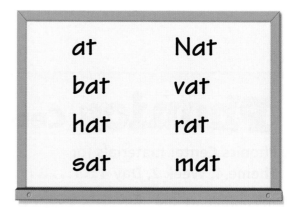

at	Nat
bat	vat
hat	rat
sat	mat

Extend Practice Extend the activity above, using *ham, sat, hat,* and *man*. Exaggerate the final sound in each word to help children name the correct final consonant. Display the sentence *I see a bat*. Children should recognize the underlined words from the Word Wall. Tell them to blend the other word to read the sentence.

Challenge

Children who can blend words with short *a* easily can begin a short *a* word bank in their journals.

INTERACTIVE WRITING
Writing Sentences

OBJECTIVES
● Write letters or words to describe illustrations.

Write a story together using action words. Review that action words tell what someone or something does. Read the posters and charts you've made together. If children have more action words to add, do it now.

● Look back at the "Best Friends" pictures children drew. Choose children to describe the actions in their illustrations.

● Then write sentences together. Tell children that complete sentences need both a noun and an action word. Guide the writing with prompts like the following.

● Maria likes to *bake*. That's a good action word. What letter shall I write first?

● How shall I start the sentence? Yes, it starts with a capital. Maria, will you write capital *M*?

> We do lots of things with our friends.
> Maria likes to bake with her mom.
> Thaddeus plays chess with his dad.
> Kendra knits potholders with her Nana.

● Who will write the word *to?* It's on our Word Wall if you need to look for it.

● Thaddeus plays chess with his dad. Thaddeus, you can write your name for us. Then I'll finish the sentence.

Continue, giving each child a chance to participate. If necessary, continue at another sitting. Children will want to read and reread their writing.

Writing Center

Materials crayons ● markers ● lined and unlined writing paper ● blank books ●

Work together to make a Best Friends Class Book. Cut the sentences from the chart. Each child can use a sentence to label his or her drawing. Bind the illustrations together to make a book. Decide on a title for the book. Choose a few children to make a sturdy cover. After you've read the book several times, put the book in the classroom library for all to read and enjoy.

DAY 5
week 2

Day at a Glance
T122–T129

Learning to Read

Revisiting the Literature, *T124*
Phonics: Review Consonants *v, h, m*; Short *a* Words, *T126*

Word Work

Building Words, *T128*

Writing & Oral Language

Independent Writing, *T129*

Daily Routines

Calendar

Reading the Calendar Review the vocabulary you have taught this week, adding *fifth* as the last word in the series. Then listen for children to incorporate these words into their oral vocabularies.

Sunday	Monday	Tuesday	Wednesday	Thursday	Friday	Saturday
			1	2	3	4
5	6	7	8	9	10	11
12	13	14	15	16	17	18
19	20	21	22	23	24	25
26	27	28	29	30	31	

third

second   *fourth*

first   *fifth*

Daily Message

Interactive Writing
When writing your daily message, have children share the pen: You can write your name, Tyrone. Here's a place for it. Put your finger after the last word to leave a space. That way, it will be easy for us to read.

We'll have cookies that Tyrone brought us.

Word Wall

High-Frequency Words Read the Word Wall together. Then play a rhyming game: I see a word that rhymes with *bat*. The word is *at*. Raise your hand when you find a word that rhymes with *me*. (see)

at	I	see	like

Word Cards for these words appear on pages R8–R9.

Daily Phonemic Awareness

Blending and Segmenting Onset and Rime

- Say: I'll say some sounds. When you know what word the sounds make, raise your hand. When most hands are raised, choose a child to pick the correct **Picture Card**.

- Choose a different picture. I'll hold up a **Picture Card**. We'll name the picture, and then you tell me the two parts that you hear. Listen: *desk*. What is the beginning sound? What is the rest of the word?

- Continue with the other cards.

Blending Phonemes

- This time I will say some separate sounds. You blend the sounds together and raise your hand when you know which card I named: /j/ /ē/ /p/. When most hands are up, ask children to say the word aloud with you. That's right! /j/ /ē/ /p/, jeep.

- Continue until all the pictures have been named.

To help children plan their day, tell them that they will–

- reread and talk about the books they've read this week.

- reread and take home "A Vat."

- write in their journals.

A Vat

by Elizabeth Kiley
illustrated by Bob Kolar

7

REVISITING THE LITERATURE
Literature Discussion

Review the week's selections, using these suggestions Ask children to think about all the books they've heard and read this week. First, help them recall the books and stories by displaying each one.

- Ask how the mouse proved that someone little can be a big help.

- Talk about how a boy and his dad can be best friends. Ask children how the book *My Dad and I* helped them find this out.

- Ask children how the people in their town or city help them. Talk about how they can be friends. Ask what the title *Friends Help Friends* means.

- Together, read "A Vat." Ask individuals how they blended *vat, mat, hat,* and *rat*.

- Go around the circle and have children tell one thing they learned from something they read or heard this week.

TARGET SKILL COMPREHENSION SKILL
Cause and Effect

Compare Books Ask children why the lion was caught in the net. Then ask why Rafa and his dad looked for a good book to read together. Remind children that it's important to think about why things happen in stories.

Rereading for Fluency

Reread Familiar Texts   Review **Phonics Library** books children have read so far. Remind them that they've learned to read the new word *to* and words with short *a*. As they reread "A Vat," have children look for words with short *a*.

- Feature several **Phonics Library** titles in the Book Corner, and have children demonstrate their growing skills by choosing one to reread aloud.

- Children can alternate pages with a partner. From time to time, ask children to point out words or pages that they can read more easily now.

Oral Reading and Retelling Stories   Frequent rereadings of familiar texts help children develop a less word-by-word and more expressive style in their oral reading. Model often how to read phrases, pausing for end punctuation. Then have children try it. Children can also practice retelling stories from earlier themes.

A Vat
by Elizabeth Kiley
illustrated by Bob Kolar

7

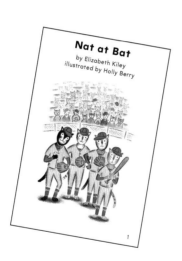

Nat at Bat
by Elizabeth Kiley
illustrated by Holly Berry

1

Assign Blackline Master 36. Children complete the page and take it home to share their reading progress. A copy appears on R12.

My Reading Log

I can read

My new words

a   to

Books for Small-Group Reading

The materials listed below provide reading practice for children at different levels.

Vocabulary Reader
What Can You Do?

Leveled Reader

Friends
by Alice Lisbon

Little Big Book

Reading
My Dad and I

by Julio Ricardo Baenga
illustrated by Joe Cepeda

Little Readers for Guided Reading

Houghton Mifflin Classroom Bookshelf

 Home Connection

Remind children to share the take-home version of "A Vat" with their families.

OBJECTIVES

- Build and read words with consonants and short *a*.
- Make sentences with high-frequency words.

Materials

- **Word Cards** *a, I, like, my, see, to*
- **Picture Cards** for sentence building
- **Punctuation Card** period

REVIEW

PHONICS
Consonants, Short *a* Words

❶ Review

Review building short *a* words. Begin by celebrating the fact that children can read many words now that they've learned about short *a* words. Display these letters on a magnetic board: *a, t, s, m, r, b, N,* and *h*. Then give children the riddle clues listed below. Children can use the magnetic letters to build the one-word answers.

- **I use this to hit my wiffle ball.** (bat)
- **This keeps my head warm.** (hat)
- **This is like a little rug.** (mat)
- **This is a boy's name.** (Nat)

HIGH-FREQUENCY WORDS
a, I, like, my, see, to

❷ Review

Review the high-frequency words from the Word Wall.

- Give each small group the **Word Cards, Picture Cards**, and **Punctuation Card** needed to make a sentence. Each child holds one card.

- Children stand and arrange themselves to make a sentence for others to read. Once children read the sentence, have them act it out.

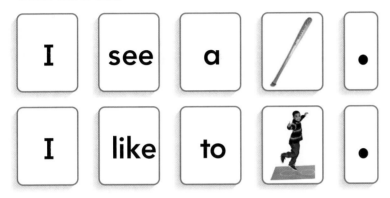

❸ Practice/Apply

- Children can complete **Practice Book** page 148 independently and read it to you during small group time.

- Pass out copies of the story *I Like My* 🏛, **Practice Book** pages 221–222. Read the title aloud. Ask children to tell who is speaking. Point to the boy and tell children that he is telling the story.

For each page, have children look at the picture and tell what the boy is doing and seeing. Have them read the page silently. Then ask a child to read the page aloud. Use questions such as the following to prompt discussion:

Pages 1–4 Where is the boy going? How does he get there? What does he see on the way? How do you get to school? What do you see along the way?

Ask children to count the high-frequency words in the story. How many times can you find the word *I* in this story? the word *see*? the word *like*? the word *to*? the word *my*? the word *a*?

Children can practice reading both high-frequency words and decodable words by rereading the **Phonics Library** story "A Vat."

Practice Book page 148

Practice Book pages 221–222

Monitoring Student Progress

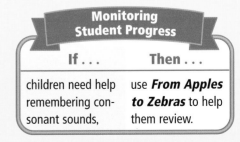

If . . .	Then . . .
children need help remembering consonant sounds,	use *From Apples to Zebras* to help them review.

High-Frequency Words   T127

PRACTICE

BUILDING WORDS
Words with Short *a*

Model building the word *vat*.

- Remind children to hold each sound as they say the next one, *ăăăt*.

- Build the word *at* in the pocket chart. Then along the bottom of a pocket chart, line up the letters *b, h, m, N, r, s,* and *v*. I want to build the word *vat, vvvăăăt*. Who can tell me which letter I should take from here to make *vvvăăăt, vat?*

- Have a child take the letter *v* and place it in front of *at*. Continue building short *a* words, using initial consonants *b, h, m, N, r,* and *s*.

- On chart paper, keep a list of all the short *a* words you make, and reread the list together.

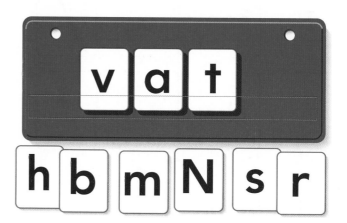

Check Understanding Have small groups work together to build short *a* words such as *vat* with magnetic letters or alphabet blocks. Show them how to make needed corrections. Children can use their new words to create and illustrate rhyming words for the Word Bank section of their journals.

Extend Practice Continue building words using *van, rat,* and *ham*. Have children blend the words. Model blending as needed. Then display the sentence *I like Nat.* Children should recognize the underlined words from the Word Wall. Tell them to blend the other word to read the sentence.

INDEPENDENT WRITING
Journals

Preparing to Write

- Place rubber stamps or stickers in the Writing Center. Stamps and stickers that are related to seasonal or holiday themes can inspire writers to write about things they like to do at this time of year.

- Journal writing is an open-ended activity, so make suggestions for topics only if children need help.

Writing Independently

- Permit children to browse through *My Dad and I* and *Friends Help Friends* for writing ideas.

- As children write their journal entries, remind them that they can use the Word Wall to help them spell words.

- For spelling help, post the Shared Writings children have completed during the week. (See page T113.) Observe children's temporary spellings to address meeting individual needs.

OBJECTIVES
- Write independently.

Materials
- journals
- **Big Book** *My Dad and I, Friends Help Friends*

DAY **5**

WRITING

WEEK 2

Portfolio Opportunity

Mark journal entries you would like to share with parents. Allow children to mark their best efforts or favorite works for sharing as well.

LEVELED READERS

WEEK 2

▲ ON LEVEL

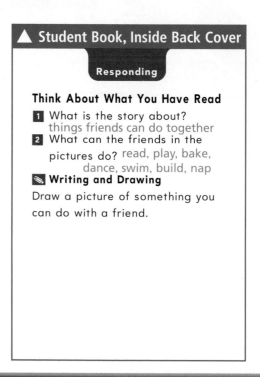

Friends

Summary: *This nonfiction book describes a variety of activities friends do together. Readers see photographs of friends reading, playing, baking, dancing, swimming, building, and napping together.*

Story Words

We *p. 2*

can *p. 2*

Building Background and Vocabulary

Tell children that this story is about the many different activities friends enjoy doing together. Preview the photographs with children. Encourage children to share their own ideas about the kinds of activities they enjoy doing with their friends. Help children make a list of the different kinds of friends they have, from their classmates to their pets and even stuffed animals.

Comprehension Skill: Cause and Effect

Read together the Strategy Focus on the book flap. Remind children to use the strategy and to think about why things happen the way they do in a story.

Responding

Discussing the Book Have children talk about their personal responses to the book. Encourage them to talk about what they liked best about the story or what they found the most interesting. Have children point to sentences or photographs they enjoyed. Ask children to compare their favorite activities to the ones shown in the book. Then help children list the different kinds of friendships portrayed in the book.

Responding Work with children to answer the questions on the inside back cover. Then help them complete the Writing and Drawing activity. Have children take turns sharing their drawings with classmates and explaining why they enjoy doing that activity with that friend. Staple the pictures together to make a class book titled *Friends*.

▲ Student Book, Inside Back Cover

Responding

Think About What You Have Read

1. What is the story about?
   things friends can do together
2. What can the friends in the pictures do? read, play, bake, dance, swim, build, nap

✎ **Writing and Drawing**

Draw a picture of something you can do with a friend.

Building Fluency

Model Reread pages 2 and 3 as children follow along in their books. Point out that the first two words, *We can*, on the two pages are the same. Tell children that these words begin every page in the book.

Practice Have children reread the same two pages several times until each child can read it aloud smoothly.

Oral Language Development

Action Words Explain that action words are words that name each action described in the story. Have children page through the story, pointing to the action word on each page (*read, play, bake, dance, swim, build, nap*). After they find each word on a page, have them look at the photograph that shows that action.

Practice Ask volunteers to pantomime each action described in the book as you reread the story aloud.

Lesson Overview

Literature

Aaron and Gayla's Alphabet Book

HOUGHTON MIFFLIN
Reading

pictures by Jan Spivey Gilchrist
written by Eloise Greenfield

ABC

Includes:
Social Studies Link

HOUGHTON MIFFLIN
Reading

My Dad and I

by Julio Ricardo Baerga
illustrated by Joe Cepeda

Includes:
Social Studies Link

1 **Teacher Read Aloud**

- *Stone Soup*

2 **Big Books**

- *Aaron and Gayla's Alphabet Book*
- *My Dad and I*

3 **Decodable Text**

Phonics Library

- "Cat Sat"

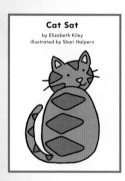

Cat Sat
by Elizabeth Kiley
illustrated by Shari Halpern

4 **Social Studies Links**

Friends Help Friends

We Read Together

These Links appear after the main
Big Book selections.

Leveled Books

Vocabulary Reader

- Below Level, ELL
- Lesson
- Take-Home Version

Leveled Reader

- On Level, Above Level
- Lesson
- Take-Home Version

Instructional Support

Planning and Practice

Planning and Classroom Management

Reading and skill instruction

Plans and activities for reaching all learners

- Newsletters
- Observation Checklists
- Theme Activity Masters

- Phonemic Awareness
- Letter Recognition
- Phonics Practice

- Independent practice for skills
- Fluency Practice: Word and Picture Books

Reaching All Learners

Coordinated lessons, activities, and projects for additional reading instruction for

- Classroom Teacher
- Extended Day
- Pull Out
- Resource Teacher

Technology

Audio Selections
Aaron and Gayla's Alphabet Book

My Dad and I

Curious George Learns Phonics

www.eduplace.com

Phonics Center

- Phonics Practice
- Word Building

Daily Lesson Plans

Technology
Lesson Planner CD-ROM allows you to customize the chart below to develop your own lesson plans.

 T Skill tested on Weekly or Theme Skills Test and/or Integrated Theme Test

60–90 minutes

Learning to Read

Phonemic Awareness

Phonics

High-Frequency Words

Comprehension

Concepts of Print

Vocabulary Reader
How to Make a Salad

Leveled Reader
A Party

DAY 1

Daily Routines, *T138–T139*
Calendar, Message, High-Frequency Words

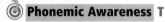 **Phonemic Awareness T**

Teacher Read Aloud, *T140–T143*

Comprehension Strategy, *T140*
Question/Evaluate

Comprehension Skill, *T140*
Cause and Effect **T**

Phonemic Awareness, *T144–T145*
Beginning Sound /k/ **T**

Leveled Reader

DAY 2

Daily Routines, *T148–T149*
Calendar, Message, High-Frequency Words

 **Phonemic Awareness T**

Reading the Big Book, *T150–T151*

Comprehension Strategy, *T150*
Evaluate

Comprehension Skill, *T150*
Text Organization and Summarizing **T**

Phonics, *T152–T153*
Initial Consonant c **T**

High-Frequency Word, *T154–T155*
Review Words: *a, to* **T**

Word and Picture Book, *T155*

Leveled Reader

30–45 minutes

Word Work

High-Frequency Word Practice

Building Words

High-Frequency Word Practice, *T146*
Words: *I, a, see, my, to*

High-Frequency Word Practice, *T156*
Building Sentences

30–45 minutes

Writing and Oral Language

Vocabulary

Writing

Listening/Speaking/Viewing

 Oral Language: Vocabulary, *T147*
Using Action Words

Vocabulary Reader

Vocabulary Reader

Vocabulary Expansion, *T157*
Using Action Words

Listening/Speaking/Viewing, *T35*

 Half-Day Kindergarten

Focus on lessons for tested skills marked with **T**. Then choose other activities as time allows.

Target Skills of the Week

Phonemic Awareness	Onset and Rime; Initial Sound /k/; Blending Phonemes
Phonics	Initial Consonant: Cc; Words with Short a
Comprehension	Cause/Effect; Text Organization; Question; Evaluate
Vocabulary	High-Frequency Words; Using Action Words
Fluency	Phonics Library; Word and Picture; Practice Reader

DAY 3

Daily Routines, T158–T159
Calendar, Message, High-Frequency Words

◉ **Phonemic Awareness** T

Reading the Big Book, T160–T161

◉ **Comprehension Strategy,** T160
Evaluate

◉ **Comprehension Skill,** T160
Cause and Effect T

◉ **Phonics,** T162
Review Initial Consonant c; Blending Short a Words T

◉ **Reading Decodable Text,** T163–T165
"Cat Sat"

Vocabulary Reader

Leveled Reader

Building Words, T166
Words with Short a

Shared Writing, T167
Writing a Note

DAY 4

Daily Routines, T168–T169
Calendar, Message, High-Frequency Words

◉ **Phonemic Awareness** T

Reading the Links: We Read Together, T170
Friends Help Friends, T171

◉ **Comprehension Strategy,** T170
Question

◉ **Comprehension Skill,** T170, T171
Text Organization and Summarizing; Cause and Effect T

◉ **Concepts of Print,** T170
Word Spacing T

◉ **Phonics,** T172–T173
Blending Short a Words T

Vocabulary Reader

Leveled Reader

Building Words, T174
Words with Short a

Interactive Writing, T175
Writing a List

DAY 5

Daily Routines, T176–T177
Calendar, Message, High-Frequency Words

◉ **Phonemic Awareness** T

Revisiting the Literature, T178

◉ **Comprehension Skill,** T178
Text Organization and Summarizing

◉ **On My Way Practice Reader,** T179

◉ **Phonics Review,** T180
Consonants, Short a Words T

High-Frequency Word Review, T181
Words: I, see, my, like, a, to T

◉ **Word and Picture Book,** T181

Vocabulary Reader

Leveled Reader

Building Words, T182
Words with Short a

Independent Writing, T183
Journals: Recording Information

Concepts of Print lessons teach important foundational skills for Phonics.

Managing Flexible Groups

Leveled Instruction and Leveled Practice

	DAY 1	**DAY 2**
WHOLE CLASS	• Daily Routines (TE pp. T138–T139) • Teacher Read Aloud: *Stone Soup* (TE pp. T140–T143) • Phonemic Awareness (TE pp. T144–T145)	• Daily Routines (TE pp. T148–T149) • Big Book: *Aaron and Gayla's Alphabet Book* (TE pp. T150–T151) • Phonics lesson (TE pp. T152–T153) • High-Frequency Word lesson (TE pp. T154–T155)
SMALL GROUPS *Organize small groups according to children's needs.*	**TEACHER-LED GROUPS** • Begin Practice Book pp. 149, 150, 151, 152. (TE pp. T141, T145) • Introduce Phonics Center. (TE p. T145) • Leveled Reader	**TEACHER-LED GROUPS** • Begin Practice Book pp. 153, 154, 155. (TE pp. T153, T155) • Write letters *C, c;* begin handwriting Blackline Master 159 or 185. (TE p. T153) • Introduce Phonics Center. (TE p. T153) • Leveled Reader • Vocabulary Reader
English Language Learners *Support is provided in the Reaching All Learners notes throughout the week.*	**INDEPENDENT GROUPS** • Complete Practice Book pp. 149, 150, 151, 152. (TE pp. T141, T145) • Use Phonics Center. (TE p. T145)	**INDEPENDENT GROUPS** • Complete Practice Book pp. 153, 154, 155. (TE pp. T153, T155) • Complete Blackline Master 159 or 185. • Use Phonics Center. (TE p. T153) • **Fluency Practice** Reread Word and Picture Book: *I Like My* 👫 . (Practice Book pp. 223–224)

• Complete Practice Book pages 149–158.

• Complete penmanship practice (Teacher's Resouce Blackline Masters 159 or 185 and 157 or 183).

• Reread familiar Phonics Library or Word and Picture Book stories.

• Share trade books from Leveled Bibliography. (See pp. T4–T5)

DAY 3

- Daily Routines (TE pp. T158–T159)
- Big Book: *My Dad and I* (TE pp. T160–T161)
- Phonics Lesson (TE p. T162)

TEACHER-LED GROUPS

- Begin Practice Book p. 156. (TE p. T162)
- Write letters *A, a*; begin handwriting Blackline Master 157 or 183.
- Read Phonics Library: "Cat Sat." (TE pp. T163–T165)
- Leveled Reader
- Vocabulary Reader

INDEPENDENT GROUPS

- Complete Practice Book p. 156. (TE p. T162)
- Complete Blackline Master 157 or 183.
- **Fluency Practice** Reread Phonics Library "Cat Sat." (TE pp. T163–T165)

DAY 4

- Daily Routines (TE pp. T168–T169)
- Social Studies Link: *Friends Help Friends* (TE p. T170)
- Social Studies Link: *We Read Together* (TE p. T171)
- Phonics lesson (TE pp. T172–T173)

TEACHER-LED GROUPS

- Begin Practice Book p. 157. (TE p. T173)
- Introduce the Phonics Center. (TE p. T173)
- **Fluency Practice** Reread Word and Picture Book: *I Like My* .
- Leveled Reader
- Vocabulary Reader

INDEPENDENT GROUPS

- Complete Practice Book p. 157. (TE p. T173)
- **Fluency Practice** Color and reread Phonics Library: "Cat Sat." (TE pp. T163–T165)
- Use Phonics Center. (TE p. T173)

DAY 5

- Daily Routines (TE pp. T176–T177)
- Rereading (TE p. T178)
- On My Way Practice Reader (TE p. T179)
- Phonics and High-Frequency Word Review (TE pp. T180–T181)

TEACHER-LED GROUPS

- Read Word and Picture Book *I Like to* .
- Begin Practice Book p. 158. (TE p. T181)
- **Fluency Practice** Reread the Take-Home version of "Cat Sat."
- Leveled Reader
- Vocabulary Reader

INDEPENDENT GROUPS

- Complete Practice Book p. 158. (TE p. T181)
- **Fluency Practice** Reread Word and Picture Book *I Like to* . Reread a favorite Phonics Library or Leveled Reader story.

- Retell or reread Little Big Books.
- Listen to Big Book Audio CDs.
- Use the Phonics Center and other Centers. (See pp. T136–T137)

Turn the page for more independent activities.

Classroom Management

Independent Activities

Assign these activities at any time during the week while you work with small groups.

Differentiated Instruction

- **Handbook for English Language Learners** pp. 134–143

- **Extra Support Handbook** pp. 130–139

Additional Independent Activities

- **Classroom Management Handbook**, pp. 90–97

- **Challenge Handbook**, pp. 30–31

⭐ Look for more activities in the **Classroom Management Kit.**

Setting Up Centers

ABC Phonics Center

Materials Phonics Center materials for Theme 4, Week 3

Children work with letters and their sounds this week. They make words with the letters *c, v, h, t,* and also short *a.* Prepare materials for the Day 1, 2, and 4 activities. Cut apart the letter grids and bag them in plastic according to color. Put out the Workmats and open the Direction Chart to the appropriate day. Follow the **Phonics Center** Routine. See pages T145, T153, and T173 for this week's **Phonics Center** activities.

Book Center

Materials books about friends

The Bibliography provides many suggestions for books about friends to add to your classroom library. If children have favorite books at home, ask them to bring them to school for their friends to share. Remind children to have clean hands before visiting the Book Center, and to observe the rules for careful book handling.

Writing Center

Materials crayons • markers • lined and unlined writing paper • blank books • grocery circulars or food advertisements ....

Children discuss action words and label pictures with these words. They also write a recipe together. Later in the week they draw and label pictures of themselves and a family member either helping or getting help. Finally, they write a list of things they want to tell people at home. See pages T141, T157, T161, and T175 for this week's Writing Center activities.

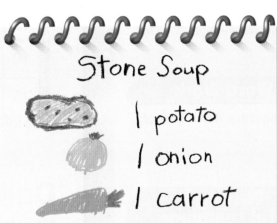

Art Center

Materials drawing paper • crayons or paints • yarn pieces ....

Children make a *Good to Eat Alphabet Book*. They cut out pictures of food items and work cooperatively to make an alphabet book. As a challenge activity, partners or small groups can make an Alphabet Book using *Aaron and Gayla's Alphabet Book* as a text model. They also make and label food collages with action words. See pages T147 or T151 for this week's Art Center activities. Put a variety of alphabet books in the Writing Center for children to use as text models.

DAY 1
week 3

Day at a Glance
T138–T147

Learning to Read

Teacher Read Aloud, *T140*
Phonemic Awareness: /k/, *T144*

Word Work

High-Frequency Word Practice, *T146*

Writing & Oral Language

Oral Language, *T147*

Daily Routines

Sunday	Monday	Tuesday	Wednesday	Thursday	Friday	Saturday
			1	2	3	4
5	6	7	8	9	10	(11)
(12)	13	14	15	16	17	18
19	20	21	22	23	24	25
26	27	28	29	30	31	

weekend

Calendar

Reading the Calendar Ask a child to point to the first day of the school week. Read the day and date for children. Point to the days that make up the weekend, and ask children to recall some things they did on Saturday and on Sunday.

Daily Message

Modeled Writing
Include some high-frequency words from the Word Wall in today's message. Ask children to point them out and underline each one.

Today <u>a</u> visitor will come <u>to</u> our class.

WELCOME

Word Wall

High-Frequency Words Read the words on the Word Wall and then play "Rhyme Time." I'm going to find a word that rhymes with *bike. Bike* rhymes with . . . *like.* Here's another word: *do.* Who can find and read a word that rhymes with *do?* Raise your hand when you find it.

like	to	see	I

Word Cards for these words appear on pages R8–R9.

⊚ Daily Phonemic Awareness

Blending and Segmenting Onset and Rime

- Read "Humpty Dumpty" on page 19 of *Higglety Pigglety*. Then discuss it, having children blend word parts: Humpty Dumpty fell off the /w/ /all/ (wall). Help was sent by the /k/ /ing/ (king).

- Have partners work together to take apart orally and put together these words: *put, sat, fall, men, wall, king.*

Blending Phonemes

- Play a guessing game. I'll say some separate sounds. You put them together to make action words: /r/ /ă/ /n/ (ran); /j/ /ŏ/ /g/ (jog); /l/ /ē/ /p/ (leap).

- Continue with other one-syllable action words.

Humpty Dumpty

Humpty Dumpty sat on a wall.
Humpty Dumpty had a great fall.
All the King's horses and
all the King's men
Couldn't put Humpty
together again.

a Mother Goose Rhyme

Higglety Pigglety: A Book of Rhymes, page 19

To help children plan their day, tell them that they will—

- listen to a story called *Stone Soup*.

- meet a new Alphafriend.

- illustrate action words in the Art Center.

- Develop oral language (listening, responding).
- Preview comprehension skill.

Read Aloud

Stone Soup

Selection Summary A young man convinces reluctant villagers to contribute potatoes, carrots, and a variety of other things to a communal "stone" soup, which he promises will be "fit for a king."

Key Concept Sharing

Show learners soup cans and a picture of a bowl of soup. Show pictures of different ingredients, and have children choose the appropriate ones for soup. Explain the meaning of the expression *fit for a king*.

Teacher Read Aloud

Building Background

Ask children what kind of soup they like. Talk about the many ingredients that go into some soups. Then read the title *Stone Soup* aloud and ask if anyone has ever heard of stone soup. Invite speculation about how stone soup might taste.

 COMPREHENSION STRATEGY

Question/Evaluate

Teacher Modeling Model the strategy as you share the title of the book and the illustration on page T143.

Think Aloud If there's something I don't understand when I read, I can ask myself a question. I know the title of this story is *Stone Soup.* That doesn't make sense to me because people don't put stones in soups. So I'll ask: What is stone soup? How is it made?

 COMPREHENSION SKILL

Cause and Effect

Teacher Modeling Remind children that thinking about why things happen helps readers understand a story, too.

Think Aloud Let's think about why someone is making stone soup. Listen as I read the story *Stone Soup.*

Listening to the Story

Hold your Teacher's Edition so that children can see page T143 as you read. Note that the art is also available on the back of the theme Poster.

Read the story aloud, helping children understand the trick that the traveler is playing. Encourage children to question why events happen.

Children who enjoyed this story may also enjoy other retellings, such as *Stone Soup* by Ann McGovern.

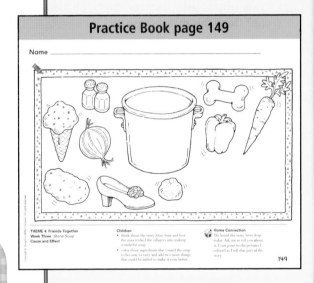

Responding

Oral Language: Retelling the Story Help children retell parts of the story.

What really is stone soup?

Did the soup taste good? How do you know?

Was the man clever? What makes you think so?

If the traveler came to your house, would your family give him things for his stone soup? Why?

Practice Book Children will complete **Practice Book** pages 149–150 during small group time.

Practice Book page 149

Name _____

Practice Book page 150

Name _____

Writing Center

Stone Soup
- 1 potato
- 1 onion
- 1 carrot

Help children recall the story together and draw the ingredients the young man put into the soup. Make an illustrated recipe. You can label the drawings. When you make the recipe with the class, children can count the ingredients.

Stone Soup

A Swedish Folk Tale

Long ago, a young man set out from his village to find work in a faraway place. He had walked for many days, and he was tired and hungry. At last, he came to a village, and he stopped at the town square where the villagers warmed themselves beside a big fire. (**Ask:** Why did the man stop in the village?)

"I am hungry," said the man to an old woman. "I'll work if you feed me."

"I am sorry, young man, but I am very poor and I have only enough food for myself," said the old woman.

The young man was disappointed, but he had an idea. He picked up a small gray stone. "Well then, may I please borrow a large kettle?" he politely asked. "I'd like to make some stone soup." (**Ask:** Whatever will the man do with a kettle and a stone? Does this make sense?)

"Soup from a stone?" said the woman. "I have never heard of it!"

"It's a secret recipe," said the man. "It makes soup fit for a king!"

The old woman laughed and said loudly so her friends could hear, "I have a kettle. Let's see you make your stone soup." The man filled the kettle and put it on the fire. He plopped the stone into the water.

"Thank you," said the young man. "This will be excellent stone soup. Now, if only I had a potato, it would be really fit for a king."

Now the woman was curious. "I might have a potato to spare." And she quickly brought the man a large, brown potato.

Then the farmer joined the group around the fire, and he asked, "What's this young man doing?"

"The traveler is making stone soup," whispered the woman. "He says it will be fit for a king!" And they smiled at each other. "Who ever heard of such a thing?" (**Ask:** What do the woman and the man think of the stranger's plan? What do you think?)

"It will be fit for a king," said the young man. "But it would be even better if I had an onion to add to the kettle."

"I have a spare onion," said the farmer. And he soon brought a large onion, which the young man tossed into the kettle.

Not long after that, the village tinsmith came along. "What's going on here?" she asked.

The woman and the farmer winked at her and said, "This young man is making stone soup. He says it will be fit for king."

The tinsmith said, "Soup from a stone? Who ever heard of it?"

"Yes, and it will be fit for a king," said the young man. "But it would be even better if I had a carrot to add to the kettle."

The tinsmith winked back at the other two and returned with a long, crispy, orange carrot. The young man chopped it and tossed it into the pot. (**Ask:** What do you think the man will ask for next?)

About this time, the village butcher was closing his shop for the day and he smelled the soup. He asked, "What's going on here?"

And the villagers answered, trying to hide their laughter, "This young man is making soup from a stone. He says it will be fit for a king."

"Soup from a stone? Who ever heard of it?" asked the butcher.

"Yes, soup from a stone," said the young man. "Now," he said. "if only I had some meat. That would make it truly fit for a king!"

By now, the butcher was laughing with the other villagers. He thought he'd join the fun too. "Meat, you say. Well, lad, I'll give you some meat for your soup." (**Ask:** What do you think of the soup now?)

Then each of the villagers found a way to join the fun. Some brought more carrots, potatoes, and celery. Some even brought barley, flour, salt, and pepper. The young man tossed everything into the boiling kettle—with the stone. And in a little while, the soup was done and there was enough for everyone in the village.

Everyone gathered around a big table in the town square. The young man served huge bowls of delicious soup. People ate until they were full. (**Ask:** Everyone shared the soup. Do you think that was a good idea? Why?)

"Soup from a stone! Well I never . . . ," said the woman. And they all congratulated the young man. "Come back again soon!" they said.

"This soup really is fit for a king!" (**Ask:** Why did the soup made with a stone taste so good?)

So the young man set off toward his home with a smile. And the villagers never found out his secret. (**Ask:** What was the young man's secret?)

OBJECTIVES

- Identify pictures whose names begin with /k/.

Materials

- **Alphafriend Cards** *Callie Cat, Hattie Horse, Vinnie Volcano*
- **Alphafriend CD** Theme 4
- **Alphafolder** *Callie Cat*
- **Picture Cards** for *c, h, v*
- **Phonics Center** Theme 4, Week 3, Day 1

Alphafolder *Callie Cat*

Show **Picture Cards** for sounds children have already learned, including some for /k/. Focus on /k/ words. Show the Alphafolder and have children name *cookies, cake, candy, cat.*

Home Connection

Hand out the take-home version of Callie Cat's song. Ask children to share the song with their families. (See **Alphafriends Blackline Masters**.)

INSTRUCTION

PHONEMIC AWARENESS
Beginning Sound

❶ Teach

Introduce the Alphafriend: Callie Cat. Use the Alphafriend routine to introduce Callie Cat.

▶ **Alphafriend Riddle** Read these clues:

- This Alphafriend is a small, furry animal. Her sound is /k/. Say it with me: /k/.

- She is cute and cuddly. She calls *meow* when she wants something.

Most children will say *cat* right away.

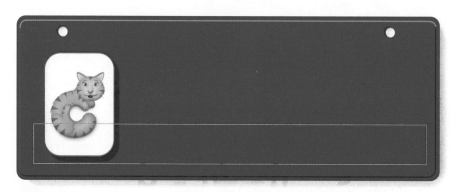

▶ **Pocket Chart** Put Callie Cat in the pocket chart. Explain that Callie's sound is /k/. Say her name, emphasizing the /k/ sound slightly, and have children echo.

▶ **Alphafriend CD** Play Callie Cat's song. Listen for words that start with /k/.

▶ **Alphafolder** Have children look at the scene and name the /k/ pictures.

▶ **Summarize**

- What is our Alphafriend's name? What is her sound?

- What words in our Alphafriend's song start with /k/?

- Each time you look at Callie Cat this week, remember the /k/ sound.

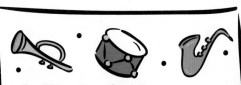

Callie Cat's Song
(tune: Yankee Doodle)

Callie Cat can bake a cake and
  cover it with candy.

Callie Cat can bake some
  cornbread. Callie is so handy.

Callie bakes some cupcakes, too.
  Her cupcakes are so cakey.

Callie bakes some cookies, too.
  Her cookies are so flakey.

❷ Guided Practice

Listen for /k/ and compare and review /v/ and /h/. Display Alphafriends *Vinny Volcano* and *Hattie Horse* opposite *Callie Cat* in the pocket chart. Review each character's sound.

Hold up the Picture Cards one at a time. Children signal "thumbs up" for words that start with Callie Cat's sound, /k/. Individuals put the cards below Callie's picture. When Callie's pictures are in place, repeat with /v/ and /h/.

Pictures: *can, cot, cow; van, vase, vet; hat, hen, hose*

Tell children that they will sort more pictures today in the **Phonics Center.**

❸ Apply

Children complete **Practice Book** pages 151–152 at small group time.

ABC Phonics Center

Materials Phonics Center materials for Theme 4, Week 3, Day 1 ....

Display Day 1 Direction Chart. Children put *Callie Cat, Vinny Volcano,* and *Hattie Horse* (without letters) in separate sections of Workmat 3. Then they sort remaining pictures by initial sound: /k/, /v/, and /h/.

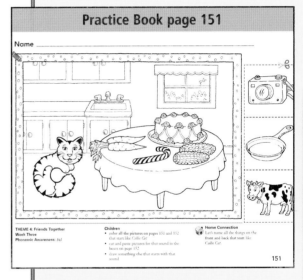

Practice Book page 151

Name _____

THEME 4: Friends Together
Week Three
Phonemic Awareness: /c/

Children
• color all the pictures on pages 151 and 152 that start like Callie Cat
• cut and paste pictures for that sound in the boxes on page 152
• draw something else that starts with that sound

Home Connection
Let's name all the things on the front and back that start like Callie Cat.

151

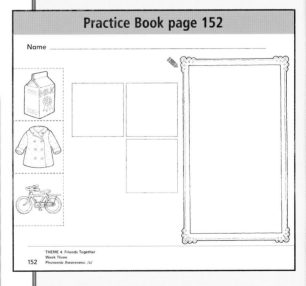

Practice Book page 152

Name _____

THEME 4: Friends Together
Week Three
152   Phonemic Awareness: /c/

OBJECTIVES

- Read high-frequency words.
- Create and write sentences with high-frequency words.

Materials

- **Word Cards** *a, I, my, see, to*
- **Picture Cards** for sentence building
- *Higglety Pigglety: A Book of Rhymes,* page 12
- **Punctuation Card** period

PRACTICE

High-Frequency Words

Display the word cards *I, a, see, my,* and *to*. As you point to each word in the pocket chart, call on children to identify it and to match it on the Word Wall.

- Remind children that these words are often seen in books. I'll read a poem. You listen carefully.

- Read "I Went Upstairs" on page 12 of *Higglety Pigglety.* Did you hear the word *I* in the poem? Let's find it. Who will match it to the **Word Card?** Children match *a, my,* and *to*.

I Went Upstairs

I went upstairs to make my bed.
I made a mistake and bumped my head.
I went downstairs to milk my cow.
I made a mistake and milked the sow.
I went to the kitchen to bake a pie.
I made a mistake and baked a fly.

a Jump-Rope Rhyme

Higglety Pigglety: A Book of Rhymes, page 12

Have children write sentences.

- Place **Word Cards** for *I, see,* and *my* in a pocket chart, along with assorted **Picture Cards** that can be used to make sentences.

- Read the words together.

- Children suggest how to make a complete sentence, adding the period. They can use the sentence stem as a model for writing.

| I | see | my | | |

TARGET SKILL

ORAL LANGUAGE: VOCABULARY
Using Action Words

- Use action words.

❶ Teach

Discuss action words.

- Remind children that action words tell what someone or something does. Give examples (*hop, run, swim, skate, chew*).

- Ask children to name some action words they know.

❷ Practice/Apply

Have children act out action words.

- Think of the action words in *Stone Soup*. Dramatize actions about soup-making such as *chop, stir,* and *peel.*

- Children can pantomime cooking actions and have others guess what they are.

Action Words

pour	stir	roll
peel	slice	measure
chop	sprinkle	bake
wash		

✏️ Writing Center

Put the list of action words in the Writing Center. Cut pictures of many kinds of foods from grocery store flyers. Children choose one picture, and use an action word to go with it. They could also paste their pictures onto drawing paper and label them.

peel

Paste

DAY 2
week 3

Day at a Glance
T148–T157

Learning to Read

Big Book, *T150*

Phonics: Initial Consonant *c, T152*

High-Frequency Words: *a, to, T154*

Word Work

High-Frequency Word Practice, *T156*

Writing & Oral Language

Vocabulary Expansion, *T157*

Daily Routines

Sunday	Monday	Tuesday	Wednesday	Thursday	Friday	Saturday
			1	2	3	4
5	6	7	8	9	10	11
12	13	14	15	16	17	18
19	20	21	22	23	24	25
26	27	28	29	30	31	

Calendar

Reading the Calendar Find and read today's date. Ask: If yesterday was *Monday,* what day i today? Yes, *Tuesday* is the second day of the school week. What's th first sound you hear in the word *Tuesday?* Point to the word *Tuesday* on the calendar.

Daily Message

Modeled Writing
Include the days of the week in your message. Have a child underline *Tuesday*.

Today is <u>Tuesday</u>.
It's Carl's turn to
feed Mr. Bunny.

Mr. Bunny

Word Wall

High-Frequency Words Whisper a word on the Word Wall to a child, and have him or her find it and read it aloud. Then have the group chant the spelling of the word: *t-o* spells *to.*

to	see	like

Word Cards for these words appear on pages R8–R9.

Daily Phonemic Awareness

Blending and Segmenting Onset and Rime

- I'll say some sounds. You put them together to name an animal: /k/ /at/ (cat); /h/ /en/ (hen).

- Continue, segmenting these words in the same way: *goat, fox, deer, pig, cow.*

- Now we'll change places. I'll name an animal and you say the beginning sound and then the rest of the word. Listen: *dog* (/d/ /og/); *cat* (/k/ /at/).

- Continue with more animal names: *fox, pig, cow, goose, yak.*

Blending Phonemes

- Now I'll say some separate sounds. You put them together to make words: /s/ /ă/ /t/ (sat); /m/ /ĕ/ /n/ (men); /h/ /ă/ /d/ (had).

- Continue with other one-syllable words.

To help children plan their day, tell them that they will—

- listen to a **Big Book**: *Aaron and Gayla's Alphabet Book.*

- learn the new letters C, c and sort words that begin with c.

- make pages for an Alphabet book in the Art Center.

OBJECTIVES

- Introduce concepts of print.
- Develop story language.
- Reinforce comprehension strategy and comprehension skill.

Big Book

Aaron and Gayla's Alphabet Book

HOUGHTON MIFFLIN
Reading

pictures by Jan Spivey Gilchrist
written by Eloise Greenfield

ABC

Includes:
Social Studies Link

Extra Support/Intervention

Display a variety of alphabet books for children to note and compare with *Aaron and Gayla's Alphabet Book*.

INSTRUCTION

Reading the Big Book

Building Background

Remind children they've heard *Aaron and Gayla's Alphabet Book* before. Tell children to listen for letters and sounds they know as you reread.

COMPREHENSION STRATEGY
Evaluate

Teacher-Student Modeling Remind children to think about how they like a book and how the book compares with others they have read.

> **Think Aloud** I really like to look at alphabet books. When I finish reading this one again, I'll think about how I liked it, and if I liked it as well as or better than other alphabet books I've read. You can do that, too.

COMPREHENSION SKILL
Text Organization and Summarizing

Teacher-Student Modeling Recall that the book is organized by the letters of the alphabet.

> **Think Aloud** I remember that knowing the alphabet helps me understand how the author wrote the book. This time, I'll think about each letter and listen for words that begin with that letter.

Concepts of Print

Word Spacing

- When I read, I know where one word ends and the next one begins by the space between them. Who can show us what I mean?

Big Book Read Aloud

Reread the story, pausing for these discussion points.

COMPREHENSION SKILL
Text Organization and Summarizing

pages 19–20

- What do Aaron and Gayla do on the *r* page? (run) What do they do on the *s* page? (sit)

Responding

Oral Language: Personal Response Have children tell what they liked best about the book. What was their favorite alphabet episode?

Practice Book Children will complete **Practice Book** page 153 during small group time.

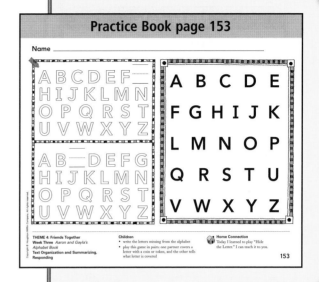

Practice Book page 153

Name _____

```
A B C D E F _
H I J K L M N
O P Q R S T _
U V W X Y Z

A B _ D E F G
H I J K L M N
O P Q R S T _
U V W X Y Z
```

```
A B C D E
F G H I J K
L M N O P
Q R S T U
V W X Y Z
```

THEME 4: Friends Together
Week Three *Aaron and Gayla's Alphabet Book*
Text Organization and Summarizing, Responding

Children
- write the letters missing from the alphabet
- play this game in pairs: one partner covers a letter with a coin or token, and the other tells what letter is covered

Home Connection
Today I learned to play "Hide the Letter." I can teach it to you.

153

Art Center

Materials pictures of foods cut from grocery flyers • Blackline Masters 70–72 ....

In the Art Center, place pictures of fruits and vegetables, cut from grocery flyers. Have children work cooperatively to make a *Good to Eat Alphabet Book*. Children paste a picture or draw a food for each letter of the alphabet. Use **Blackline Masters** 70–72 for alphabet pages if you wish.

Challenge

Groups of children may wish to make their own alphabet books with an activity for each letter. They can use *Aaron and Gayla's Alphabet Book* as a model.

BIG BOOK

Aaron and Gayla's Alphabet Book

- Identify words that begin with /k/.
- Identify pictures whose names start with the letter *c*.
- Form the letters *C, c*.

- **Alphafriend Card** *Callie Cat*
- **Letter Cards** *c, h,* and *v*
- **Picture Cards** for *c, h,* and *v*
- **Blackline Master** 159
- **Phonics Center** Theme 4, Week 3, Day 2

Callie Cat's Song

(tune: Yankee Doodle)

Callie Cat can bake a cake and
  cover it with candy.

Callie Cat can bake some
  cornbread. Callie is so handy.

Callie bakes some cupcakes, too.
  Her cupcakes are so cakey.

Callie bakes some cookies, too.
  Her cookies are so flakey.

 PHONICS
Initial Consonant *c*

❶ Phonemic Awareness Warm-Up

Beginning Sound Read or sing the lyrics from "Callie Cat's Song," and have children sing along. Have them listen for the /k/ words and raise their hands each time they hear one. See Theme Resources page R4 for music and lyrics.

❷ Teach Phonics

Beginning Letter Display the *Callie Cat* card, and have children name the letter on the picture. The letter *c* usually stands for the sound /k/, as in *cat*. You say /k/. When you see *Callie Cat,* remember the letter *c*. That will help you remember the sound /k/.

Write *cat* on the board. Underline the *c*. What is the first letter in the word *cat*? (c) *Cat* starts with /k/, so *c* is the first letter I write for *cat*.

❸ Guided Practice

Compare and Review: *v, h* In a pocket chart, display the **Letter Cards** as shown and the **Picture Cards** in random order. Review the sounds for *c, v,* and *h*. In turn, children can name a picture, say the beginning sound, and put the card below the right letter. Tell children they will sort more pictures in the **Phonics Center** today.

<table>
<tr><td>

**Penmanship
Rhyme: C**

Start near the top line.
Curve around.
Make a half circle,
nice and round.

</td><td>

**Penmanship
Rhyme: c**

Start near the mid line.
Curve around.
Leave the circle open,
but nice and round.

</td></tr>
</table>

Penmanship: Writing C, c Tell children that now they'll learn to write the letters that stand for /k/: capital C and small c. Trace each letter as you recite the penmanship rhyme. Children chant each rhyme as they "write" the letter in the air.

❹ Apply

Have children complete **Practice Book** page 154 at small group time.

For additional penmanship practice, assign **Blackline Master** 159. Penmanship practice for continuous stroke style is available on **Blackline Master** 185.

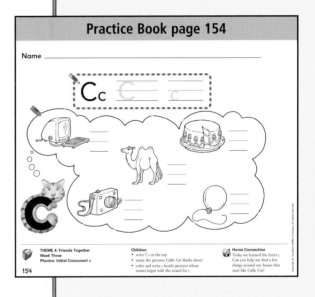

Practice Book page 154

ABC Phonics Center

Materials Phonics Center materials for Theme 4, Week 3, Day 2 · · · · · · · · · · · · · ·

Display Day 2 Direction Chart. Children put *Callie Cat, Vinnie Volcano,* and *Hattie Horse* (with letters) in separate sections of Workmat 3. Then they sort remaining pictures by initial letter: *c, v,* and *h.*

Extra Support/ Intervention

To help children remember how to form the letter *c,* point out that the letter's shape is half a circle.

OBJECTIVES

- Read and write the high-frequency words *a, to.*

Materials

- **Word Cards** *a, I, like, my, to, see*
- **Picture Cards** *dog, hug, map*
- **Punctuation Card** *period*
- **Teacher-made word card** *hat*

HIGH-FREQUENCY WORDS
Review Words: *a, to*

❶ Teach

Remind children that they have learned two new words, *a* and *to*. Tell them that today they will practice reading and writing *a* and *to*.

- Say *to* and choose a child to use it in a sentence.
- Write *to* on the board. Children spell it aloud. Spell *to* with me, *t-o, to.*
- Have one child lead the others in a chant, clapping on each beat: *t-o, to! t-o, to!*
- Repeat for the word *a*, reminding children that *a* is both a letter and a word.

Word Wall Have children find the new words on the Word Wall. Remind them to use the Word Wall to spell the words correctly.

❷ Guided Practice

Build sentences one at a time. First, make a word card for *hat*. Then create these sentences in a pocket chart. Choose several children to read them aloud. Place the pocket chart in the Writing Center. Add a few more **Picture Cards** so that children can practice building and reading sentences.

Practice reading *a*, *to*, *like*, and *my* in a poem.

- Print the following rhyme on chart paper and read it aloud for children.

- Reread the rhyme, tracking the print. Point to *a* and *to* in the first line, and call on children to find those words each time they appear.

> I'd like a cat to stay by my side.
>
> I'd like a dog to run with and hide.
>
> I'd like a bird to fly around inside.
>
> But all I can have is a bike to ride.

- Use the poem to review *like* and *my*.

❸ Apply

- Have children complete **Practice Book** page 155 at small group time. They will read and write *a* and *to* as they complete the page.

- Pass out copies of *I Like My* 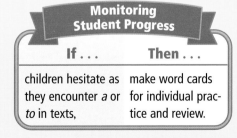 on **Practice Book** pages 223–224. Read the title aloud. Ask children to tell who is speaking. Point to the girl and tell children that she is telling the story.

For each page, have children look at the picture and tell what the child sees. Have them read the page silently. Then ask an individual to read the page aloud. Use questions such as the following to prompt discussion:

Pages 1–3 Whom is the girl visiting? What does she see at her grandparents' house? What does she do there?

Pages 4 What does she say about her grandparents? Whom do you like to visit?

Ask children to count the high-frequency words in the story: How many times can you find the word *I* in this story? the word *see*? the word *like*? the word *to*? the word *my*? the word *a*?

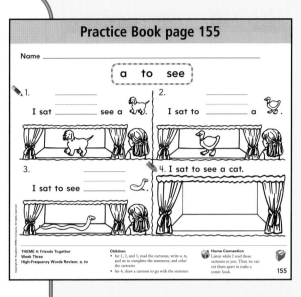

Practice Book page 155

Practice Book pages 223–224

OBJECTIVES

- Read high-frequency words.
- Create and write sentences with high-frequency words.

Materials

- **Word Cards** *a, I, like, my, see, to*
- **Picture Cards** *bike, cat, dog, run*
- **Punctuation Card** *period*

High-Frequency Words

Display all the Word Cards and Picture Cards in random order. Tell children they will write about things they like.

- I'll start writing *I like.* . . . Who can put those words on the chart? Who will add our new word *to?* Let's read what we have so far. How will we finish our sentence? What mark will we put at the end?

- Read the completed sentence together. Then continue with a new one.

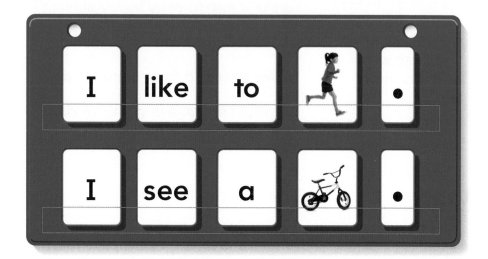

Have children write sentences of their own. Encourage children to use the high-frequency words they know. Remind children to use what they know about letters and sounds to write words they want to spell.

TARGET SKILL

VOCABULARY EXPANSION
Using Action Words

Listening/Speaking/Viewing

Review action words. Remind children of what they have learned about action words.

- Tell them that today they'll talk about what they like best to do in the classroom. Give a few examples: At the Writing Center, we draw, color, and write. In the block corner, we build. What do we do in the Art Center? at music time?

- Record children's responses.

More Action Words

build	draw
color	write
sing	paint
run	play

🎨 Art Center

Materials drawing paper • crayons or paints • yarn pieces ....

Put the list of action words in the Writing Center. Children can choose an action word to illustrate. They can also label their picture.

OBJECTIVES

- Use action words.

Vocabulary Support

The Vocabulary Reader can be used to develop and reinforce vocabulary related to the instruction for this week.

Vocabulary Reader

HOUGHTON MIFFLIN
Vocabulary Readers

How to Make a Salad
by Michele Perreault • illustrated by Renée Daily

REACHING ALL LEARNERS

English Language Learners

Ask learners to think of things they like to do in school. Have them share with a partner. Write on the board: [name] likes to ____. I like to ____. Fill in the blanks to model the activity. Ask individuals to repeat the two sentences together for the whole class, using their friends' names.

Day at a Glance
T158–T167

Learning to Read

Big Book, *T160*
Phonics: Reviewing Consonant *c;*
Blending Short *a* Words, *T162*

Word Work

Building Words, *T166*

Writing & Oral Language

Shared Writing, *T167*

Daily Routines

Sunday	Monday	Tuesday	Wednesday	Thursday	Friday	Saturday
			1	2	3	4
5	6	7	8	9	10	11
12	13	14	15	16	17	18
19	20	21	22	23	24	25
26	27	28	29	30	31	

Calendar

Reading the Calendar Have children count to three and fin the third day of the school week. Name the day and date for children. If there is a holida or vacation day approaching, point that out and count the days until the date.

Daily Message

Interactive Writing Write about an upcoming event. Have children contribute to the message. Choose children to write a high-frequency word or to write their names.

> We will go to the turkey farm on Friday.
>
> Kara wants to look for a brown turkey.

Word Wall

High-Frequency Words Play "Pass the Pointer" with the Word Wall words. Say a word and pass the pointer to a child. That child finds the word, reads it, and passes the pointer to another child. Say a different word for that child to find.

I   see

my   like   a

Word Cards for these words appear on pages R8–R9.

Daily Phonemic Awareness

Blending and Segmenting Onset and Rime

- Recite "Humpty Dumpty" from *Higglety Pigglety* several times with children.

- Now I'll change a word. Blend the sounds and raise your hand when you know my new word.

- Recite the rhyme, replacing a word with sounds for children to blend, for example: "Humpty Dumpty sat on a /w/ /all/ (wall)."

- Play again, pausing for children to segment words.

Blending Phonemes

- Now I'll say some separate sounds. You put them together: /h/ /ŏ/ /t/ (hot). Continue with *egg, men,* and *sat.*

Humpty Dumpty

Humpty Dumpty sat on a wall.
Humpty Dumpty had a great fall.
All the King's horses and
all the King's men
Couldn't put Humpty
together again.

a Mother Goose Rhyme

Higglety Pigglety: A Book of Rhymes,
page 19

Getting Ready to Learn

To help children plan their day, tell them that they will—

- reread and talk about the **Big Book**: *My Dad and I.*

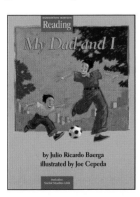

- read a story called "Cat Sat."

- explore what we know about family and friends.

OBJECTIVES

- Recognize concepts of print.
- Develop story language.
- Reinforce comprehension strategy and comprehension skill.

Big Book

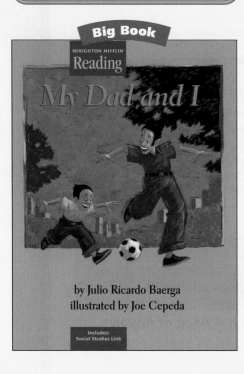

HOUGHTON MIFFLIN
Reading

My Dad and I

by Julio Ricardo Baerga
illustrated by Joe Cepeda

Includes:
Social Studies Link

Challenge

For children who seem to have a good sense of story, have them add more episodes to the **Big Book.** They can share them orally or illustrate their ideas.

INSTRUCTION

Reading the Big Book

Building Background

Browse through the **Big Book** *My Dad and I* to prompt children to tell what they remember of the story. Now read it again.

COMPREHENSION STRATEGY

Evaluate

Student Modeling Say that *My Dad and I* is about a boy and his dad—just like the people children may have in their own lives.

Think Aloud Let's think about what Rafa and his dad do together. How is it like the things you do in your own family? Does this help you feel as if you know Rafa and his dad a little better? How?

COMPREHENSION SKILL

Cause and Effect

Student Modeling Remind children that knowing what caused something to happen helps readers understand a story. Sometimes asking *why* helps us understand.

Think Aloud We read that Rafa and his dad are best friends. Let's ask ourselves why they love each other.

Big Book Read Aloud

Reread the story, pausing for these discussion points.

COMPREHENSION SKILL
Cause and Effect

page 4

- **Why do you think Rafa is getting better at soccer?** (His dad is teaching him.) **How else can you get better at something?** (by practicing)

COMPREHENSION STRATEGY
Evaluate

pages 1–18

- The author wrote about very ordinary things that are special to Rafa and his dad. What do you think about that? What did you like about it?

Responding

Oral Language: Literature Circle Have children talk about Rafa and his dad. How is their friendship special? Is Rafa a good son? Is his dad fun?

Materials drawing paper • crayons or markers

Tell children that grown-ups or family members can be very best friends who help each other. Ask each child to draw and label a picture of himself or herself helping or getting help from a family member.

 **Portfolio Opportunity**

Add children's drawings of their families to their portfolios. Share the pictures with parents at conference time.

Monitoring Student Progress

If . . .	Then . . .
children need more practice recognizing cause-effect relationships,	ask *Why* questions and have children respond with *Because* answers.

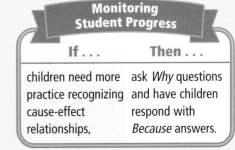

OBJECTIVES

- Identify words with initial consonant *c*, /k/.
- Blend and read words with *b, c, h, m, N, r, s, v* and short *a*.

Materials

- **Alphafriend Cards** *Andy Apple, Callie Cat*
- **Letter Cards** *a, b, c, h, m, N, r, P, S, s, t, v*
- **Alphafriend CD** Theme 4
- **Blending Routines Card 1**

Practice Book page 156

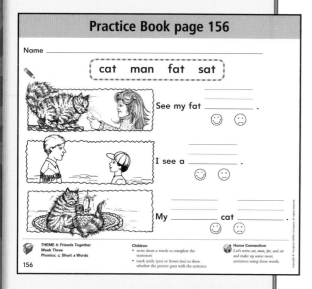

Monitoring Student Progress

If . . .	Then . . .
children have trouble blending words such as *mat*, *sat*, and *can*,	repeat this lesson using **Blending Routines Card 2**, *Sound-by-Sound Blending.*

PHONICS

Blending Short *a* Words

❶ Teach: Connect Sounds to Letters

Review consonant c. Ask children what letter and sound they think of when they see Callie Cat.

- Play Callie Cat's song. Children clap for each /k/ word.

Introduce short a. Tell children they'll build a word with *c*, but first they'll need a vowel ("helper letter").

- Display and review **Alphafriend** *Andy Apple.* You remember Andy Apple. Andy's letter is the vowel *a*, and the sound *a* usually stands for is /ă/. Say /ă/ with me, /ă/, /ă/, /ă/.

- Hold up the **Letter Card** *a*. You say /ă/. Listen for the /ă/ sound in these words: /ă/ *apple*, /ă/ *ask*, /ă/ *after*.

Model Blending Routine 1. Now show the **Letter Cards** *a* and *t*. Have children identify each letter and its sound.

- Model blending the sounds as you point to each letter with a sweeping motion. I say the sounds in order: first /ă/, then /t/. I hold each sound until I say the next one, *aăăăt, at*. I've made the word *at*. Repeat, having children blend and pronounce *at* with you.

- Show **Letter Cards** *c, a,* and *t*. Model blending the sounds as you point to the letters with a sweeping motion: *căăăt, cat*. Repeat, having children blend *cat* with you and on their own.

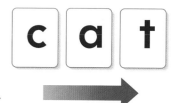

- Repeat this procedure with *bat*. Then display *hat, rat,* and *Nat* and have children blend the sounds as you point to the letters.

❷ Guided Practice

Check Understanding Display the word *sat* and ask individuals to blend the word. For more practice display *mat, can, man, van,* and *vat*. Have children blend the words, modeling blending as needed. Continue as children blend these words: *ham, Sam, pat, Nan*. Display the sentence I *see* my *bat*. (The underlined words are from the Word Wall.) Tell them to blend the other word to read the sentence.

❸ Apply

Children complete **Practice Book** page 156 at small group time.

Cat Sat

by Elizabeth Kiley
illustrated by Shari Halpern

13

Friends Together

PHONICS LIBRARY
Reading Decodable Text

Phonics/Decoding Strategy

Teacher-Student Modeling Discuss using the Phonics/Decoding strategy to read words in the story.

Think Aloud Let's read the title. I see a word I know—*cat.* I see a cat on the page, too. The next word begins with *S.* The sound for *S* is /s/. And look! The other letters are *a* and *t.* I blend the letters to read this word: *sssăăăt, sat.*

Preview the pictures on pages 14–15. Ask what the cat is holding. (a mat, something to sit on) Ask children to say *cat, mat,* and point out that the words rhyme. Ask them to predict what other things the cat might have in this story.

See my cat.

14

cat mat

15

Prompts for Decoding

Have children read each page silently before they read aloud to you. Remind children to look at each letter as they sound out the word. Prompts:

page 15 Point out the mat on page 15. Write *mat* on the board. Model blending the sounds: *mmmăăăt, mat.* Remind children to hold each sound until they say the next one. Ask one child to point and model blending.

page 16 What is the cat sitting on? Show me the word that tells you what the cat is sitting on. What is the cat holding? Show me the word that tells you what the cat is holding.

page 17 What word rhymes with *cat*? What letters are the same in these words?

Word Key

Decodable words with short *a* _____

High-Frequency Words _____

cat hat
cat bat

16

My cat sat.
Cat!

17

Oral Language

Discuss the story. Remind children to speak in complete sentences.

- Ask children to describe the cat on page 15. Encourage descriptions that include color, size, and shape words.
- Then have children describe the cat, using the descriptive words in sentences.
- Point out that the name for Cat's things are rhyming words: *cat mat, cat hat, cat bat.*

Identify rhyming words. Ask children to reread the story and identify rhyming words. *(cat, mat, hat, bat, sat)* Then ask children to model blending the words. Remind them to hold each sound until they say the next one. Then have children name other things that would also rhyme with these words.

Build Fluency

Model fluent reading.

- Read aloud page 17. Then have children read the page aloud.
- Have children reread the same page several times until each child can read it aloud smoothly.

Home Connection

Have children color the pictures in the take-home version of "Cat Sat." After rereading on Day 4, they can take it home to read it to family members. (See **Phonics Library Blackline Masters**.)

PRACTICE

BUILDING WORDS
Words with Short *a*

Model building the word *at*.

- Display the **Letter Cards** *a, b, c, h, m, r, s, t,* and *v*.

- Listen to the word *at*. I'll say the sounds slowly and we can write the word together: /ă/ /t/. How many sounds do you hear? The first sound is /ă/. What letter stands for /ă/? Put the **Letter Card** *a* in the chart. The next sound is /t/. What letter should I use? Add the **Letter Card** *t* next to the *a*. We wrote *at*.

Model building words that rhyme with *at*.

- Now let's write *cat, căăăt*. How many sounds do you hear? The first sound is /k/. What letter stands for /k/? Put the **Letter Card** *c* in the chart. The next sound is /ă/. What letter should I use? Continue with the final sound in *cat*.

- Repeat the procedure to write *mat*.

- Then have children write these words on white boards as you coach them: *sat, hat, bat, vat*.

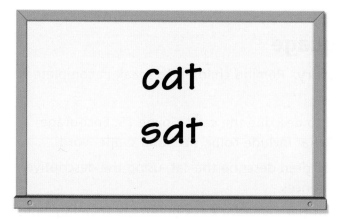

Word Wall Have a child point to *at* on the Word Wall. Remind children that they can use *at* to help them read and write words that rhyme with *at*.

Check Understanding Ask children to write the word *mat* on their white boards. Show them how to make needed corrections.

Extend Practice Continue the above procedure, mixing spelling patterns by using these words: *mat, man, sat, van, hat, can, cat, rat, ran*. Continue, adding these words: *cab, ban, tab, ham, Sam, tan*. Then display the sentence *I see my cat*. (The underlined words are from the Word Wall.) Tell children to read the underlined words without sounding them out, and to blend the other word to read the sentence.

SHARED WRITING
Writing a Note

OBJECTIVES
- Participate in a shared writing activity.
- Use action words.

DAY
3

WRITING

WEEK 3

Prepare to write a note together.

- Remind children that action words can make their writing more interesting.
- Invite children to brainstorm some action words.

Write a note together.

- Write a note to someone that the children know. Use the shared writing experience to reinforce writing conventions.
- How shall we start the note? Mrs. Morales's name starts like Mike's name. What letter stands for that sound?
- *Spin* is a great action word. Let's use it in our note.
- How shall we end our note?
- Children can sign their names to the note. Remind them to use their best handwriting.

Dear Mrs. Morales,

Thank you for teaching us how to dance.
We like to spin and tap our shoes together.

Your friends,
Mr. Taylor's class

Shana   Eric
Jacob   Bobby
      Sam
Tanya   Maria
          Eliza

Day at a Glance
T168–T175

Learning to Read

Big Books, *T170*

Phonics: Reviewing Consonant *c*; Blending Short *a* Words, *T172*

Word Work

Building Words, *T174*

Writing & Oral Language

Interactive Writing, *T175*

Daily Routines

Sunday	Monday	Tuesday	Wednesday	Thursday	Friday	Saturday
			1	2	3	4
5	6	7	8	9	10	11
12	13	14	15	16	17	18
19	20	21	22	23	24	25
26	27	28	29	30	31	

Calendar

Reading the Calendar As you do your calendar routine, count down the days until a holiday or special event.

Daily Message

Modeled Writing
Use the daily message to help children understand the practical reasons for writing. A list can often illustrate the point.

Don't Forget
permission slips
warm mittens
hat
boots

Word Wall

High-Frequency Words Play "I Spy" with the words on the Word Wall. I spy word that has three letters. It begins with /s/ and rhymes with *knee*. (see) Continue with similar clues for other words.

see	my	to

Word Cards for these words appear on pages R8–R9.

Daily Phonemic Awareness

Blending and Segmenting Onset and Rime

- Read "Rainy Day" on page 13 of *Higglety Pigglety*.
- Play a word sound game. I'll say some sounds. You put them together to make words from the poem: /r/ . . . /oad/ *(road)*; /w/ . . . /ish/ *(wish)*.
- Now I'll say a word, and you take it apart: *toes*. Say the beginning sound and then the rest of the word. (/t/ . . . /oes/)
- Continue with other one-syllable words from the poem.

Blending Phonemes

- Play "Pat, Pat, Clap" to name words from the poem.
- Slowly pat *three* times with children as you say: /w/ /ĕ/ /t/; they clap and say *wet* on the fourth beat.
- Continue with other words from "Rainy Day."

Rainy Day

I do not like a rainy day.
The road is wet, the sky is gray.
They dress me up, from head to toes,
In lots and lots of rubber clothes.
I wish the sun would come and stay.
I do not like a rainy day.

by William Wise

13

Higglety Pigglety: A Book of Rhymes,
page 13

Getting Ready to Learn

To help children plan their day, tell them that they will–

- reread the **Big Books**: *We Read Together* and *Friends Help Friends*.

- learn to write and read new words.

- read a book called "Cat Sat."

Cat Sat
by Elizabeth Kiley
illustrated by Shari Halpern

13

OBJECTIVES

- Recognize text organization.
- Recognize cause and effect.
- Match spoken words to print.

Big Book

We Read Together
Social Studies Link

Aaron and Gayla's
Alphabet Book
pictures by Jan Spivey Gilchrist
written by Eloise Greenfield

READING THE BIG BOOKS
Social Studies Link

Building Background

Rereading for Understanding Display the title page for *We Read Together* and read the title aloud. Ask children to tell what they remember about it.

- Say that some books tell stories. Others give information. **Does this part of the book tell a story or give information? How do you know?** (It gives information. It's about real people and things. We can tell from the pictures.)

- Share the selection, pausing for discussion points.

COMPREHENSION STRATEGY
Question

pages 31–37

- **What big question did we have to answer as we reread this book?** (What do people read together?)

COMPREHENSION SKILL
Text Organization and Summarizing

pages 31–37

- **Each page of this article shows people reading. How does this help you answer your question?** (It tells about things people read together.)

Concepts of Print

pages 34–35

- **Word Spacing** Reread the sentence on page 34, and have children tell how many words are in it. Ask: **How do you know?** Then choose a child to demonstrate the answer for the sentence on page 35.

Responding

Oral Language: Text Innovation Children can add to the book by listing more things they read. We read a sign, . . . a chart, . . . a calendar, . . . a job list.

Extra Support/Intervention

Let pairs of children revisit each article together. They tell each other what they liked, using the pictures as prompts.

READING THE BIG BOOKS
Social Studies Link

Building Background

Rereading for Understanding Now take a look at *Friends Help Friends*. Ask if it's a story or an informational article. Ask: **How do you know?** Reread, pausing for discussion as you share the selection.

COMPREHENSION SKILL
Cause and Effect

page 22

- Why do children need teachers at school?

CRITICAL THINKING
Guiding Comprehension

page 23

- **MAKING JUDGEMENTS** Did this article make you think about the people who help you? How?

Responding

Oral Language: Evaluate Have children tell something they learned from this book. Then talk about the author's role. If you were the author and could add another page to this book, what job would you tell about? Where is the job? Who is the helper?

Challenge

Some children may wish to use *Friends Help Friends* to start a scrapbook of local heroes, people in the community who help others.

OBJECTIVES

- Identify initial *c* for words that begin with /k/.
- Blend and read words with consonants and short *a*.

Materials

- *From Apples to Zebras: A Book of ABC's,* page 4
- **Alphafriend Card** *Andy Apple*
- **Letter Cards** *a, b, c, h, m, N, r, S, t, v*
- **Phonics Center** Theme 4, Week 3, Day 4
- **Blending Routines Card 1**

Home Connection

Have children look in their kitchens for items or for names that begin with the consonant *c*. Children can draw pictures to show what they have found.

PHONICS
Blending Short *a* Words

Review consonant *c*. On page 4 of *From Apples to Zebras*, cover the words with self-stick notes. Then display the page.

- Ask what letter children expect to see first in each word and why.
- Uncover the words so that children can check their predictions.

From Apples to Zebras: A Book of ABC's, page 4

Review short *a*. Review with children that in order to build a word with *c*, they need a vowel ("helper letter") because every word has a vowel.

- Ask which Alphafriend stands for the vowel sound /ă/.
- Display Andy Apple, and have children name other words that start with /ă/. *(ant, animal, and, act)*

Review Blending Routine 1. Hold up **Letter Cards** *a* and *t*.

- Watch and listen as I build a word from the Word Wall: /ă//t/, ăăăt, at.
- Put **Letter Card** *c* in front of *at*. Now let's blend my new word: /k//a//t/, căăăt, cat.
- Continue, choosing children to build and read *bat, hat, mat, rat, sat,* and *vat.*

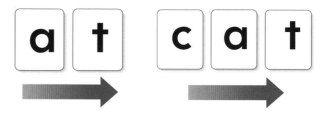

Check Understanding Display the word *vat* and ask individuals to blend the word. For more practice, display *hat, tan,* and *mat* and have children blend the words, modeling blending as needed. Remind children to hold each sound until they say the next one. Continue as children blend the following: *van, Sam, man.* Display the sentence *I like my hat.* (The underlined words are from the Word Wall.) Have children read it, blending the sounds for the last word.

Practice/Apply In a pocket chart, display the **Picture Card** for *cat*.

Have children say *cat* with you.

Then have children build the word *cat* in a pocket chart.

Repeat with *hat* and *bat*. Individuals read the words and use each one in an oral sentence.

Have children complete **Practice Book** page 157 at small group time.

In groups today, children will read short *a* words as they reread the **Phonics Library** story "Cat Sat." See suggestions, pages T163–T165.

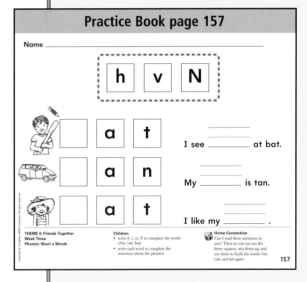

Practice Book page 157

ABC Phonics Center

Materials Phonics Center materials for Theme 4, Week 3, Day 4

Display Day 4 Direction Chart and Workmat 4. Children place a **Picture Card** (*cat, hat,* or *vat*) in the first box and then build the word with **Letter Cards,** sound by sound. In the same way, they build the other short *a* words.

Monitoring Student Progress

If . . .	Then . . .
children frequently ask how to spell short *a* words,	have them make a personal short *a* word bank.
children can easily build and blend short *a* words,	have them write sentences using the words.

OBJECTIVES

- Blend consonants with short *a* to read words.

Materials

- Letter Cards *a, b, c, h, m, N, r, s, t, v*

BUILDING WORDS
Words with Short *a*

Model building the word *cat*.

- Display **Letter Cards** *a, b, c, h, m, N, r, s, t,* and *v*.

- How many sounds do you hear in *cat?* The first sound is /k/. I'll put up a *c* to spell that. What letter stands for the middle sound, /ă/? I'll add an *a* to spell that. The last sound is /t/. What letter stands for that sound? I'll add a *t* to spell that sound.

- Now I'm going to say a word. I'll ask you to build what I say. Listen: *mat*.

- Continue with *hat, vat, rat, cat,* and *sat*.

Play a rhyming game. Tell children that Mr. and Mrs. Cat have many children in their family. All the children like to play rhyming games. One day they wrote words that rhymed with *cat*.

- Ask children to brainstorm a list that the cats might have written.

- Have individuals write words that rhyme with *cat* on the board.

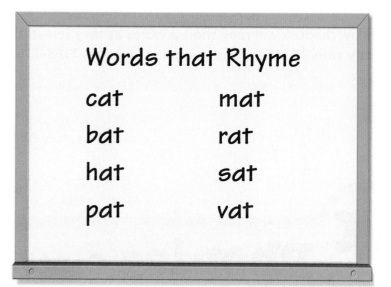

Words that Rhyme

cat	mat
bat	rat
hat	sat
pat	vat

Check Understanding Ask children to write the word *hat* on their white boards. Show children how to make needed corrections.

Extend Practice Use the words *ham, vat, van,* and *man*. Exaggerate the final sound in each word to help children name the correct final consonant. Display the sentence *I see my hat*. (Underlined words are from the Word Wall). Have children read it, blending the sounds for the last word.

Extra Support/ Intervention

Make flash cards for short *a* words with initial consonants in a different color. Partners can take turns reading the words to each other.

INTERACTIVE WRITING
Writing a List

Write a list together.

- Remind children of the list you wrote for the Daily Message. Tell them that they can write lists, too.

- Explain that lists can help remind people of jobs to be done, phone calls to be made, items to buy, and so on. Make a list of jobs to be done in your classroom, and have children share the pen as you write.

- We can call our list a "To Do" list because it reminds us of things we have to do. Who will write the word *To?* If you're not sure how to spell it, where will you look?

- *Feed,* that's a good action word.

- Who knows what letter stands for the first sound in *Mr.?* Who will write it for us?

- *Stack,* that's another action word. Good! Let's use it.

- Post your "To Do" list and have children refer to it. Whenever possible, add pictures as visual clues.

To Do

1. Feed Mr. Bunny.

2. Water the plants.

3. Stack the blocks.

4. Put away the crayons.

Writing Center

Have each child make a list of things he or she wants to tell someone at home tonight. Children can draw or write their lists.

Day at a Glance
T176–T183

Learning to Read

Revisiting the Literature, *T178*
Phonics Review: Consonants *h,
v, c;* Short *a* Words, *T180*

Word Work

Building Words, *T182*

Writing &
Oral Language

Independent Writing, *T183*

Daily Routines

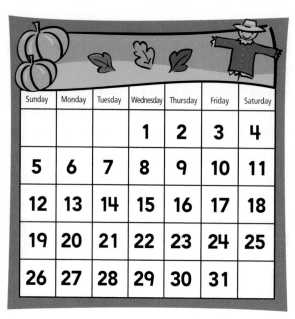

Sunday	Monday	Tuesday	Wednesday	Thursday	Friday	Saturday
			1	2	3	4
5	6	7	8	9	10	11
12	13	14	15	16	17	18
19	20	21	22	23	24	25
26	27	28	29	30	31	

Calendar

Reading the Calendar Help
children find the date on the
calendar. Have them count the
number of days in a weekend.
Name *Saturday* and *Sunday,*
asking them what they notice.
They might note the beginning
letters or the small word *day.*

Daily Message

Modeled Writing
Use the calendar
discussion as a basis
for the Daily Message.

Tomorrow is
Saturday. Miguel is
going to visit his
friend José.

Word Wall

High-Frequency Words
Have children take turns
reading Word Wall words.
Then choose a child to point
as others read the word.

I   see

my   like   to

Word Cards for these words appear on pages R8–R9.

Daily Phonemic Awareness

Blending and Segmenting Onset and Rime

- Play "Pat, Pat, Clap." Pat and clap with children as you say: /qu/ . . . /it/, *quit*; /b/ . . . /ag/, *bag*.

- Now I'll say a word. You "pat, pat" the beginning sound and the rest of the word, then "clap" to say the word again. Listen: *fit*. (/f/ . . . /it/, *fit*)

- Continue with other words from the list.

Blending Phonemes

- Say: I'll say some sounds. You put them together to make a word. Listen: /m//ī/ . . . That's right, *my*. Say the sounds with me: /m//ī/, *my*.

- Continue with other one-syllable words. Choose words with two to four sounds.

More Words for		
Pat	Pat	Clap
pin	kid	not
sip	fun	miss
bus	top	vet
ham	hat	van

Getting Ready to Learn

To help children plan their day, tell them that they will—

- talk about the books they've read in *Friends Together*.

- take home a story they can read.

Cat Sat
by Elizabeth Kiley
illustrated by Shari Halpern

- write in their journals.

You can write about:

cars
pets
football
a trip
dinosaurs

Aaron and Gayla's Alphabet Book
pictures by Jan Spivey Gilchrist
written by Eloise Greenfield

HOUGHTON MIFFLIN
Reading

Includes:
Social Studies Link

Cat Sat
by Elizabeth Kiley
illustrated by Shari Halpern

13

HOUGHTON MIFFLIN
Reading

My Dad and I

by Julio Ricardo Baerga
illustrated by Joe Cepeda

Includes:
Social Studies Link

REVIEW

REVISITING THE LITERATURE
Literature Discussion

Review the week's selections, using these suggestions.

● Ask how the young man tricked the villagers in *Stone Soup*. (He talked them into giving food to put in his soup.)

● Ask what special kind of book Aaron and Gayla's is. (alphabet book)

● Have children hold up *We Read Together* and describe what each child is reading.

● Call on individuals to tell who helps in *Friends Help Friends*.

● Have children talk about what Rafa and his father did together in *My Dad and I*.

● Together, read parts of "Cat Sat."

TARGET SKILL COMPREHENSION SKILL
Text Organization and Summarizing

Compare Books Remind children that some books tell stories and some give information. Have children work together to decide which category each book or article belongs to. Help children see that informational texts such as *We Read Together, Friends Help Friends,* and *Friends at School* are organized by showing photographs and captions or labels that describe the photos. *Aaron and Gayla's Alphabet Book* is organized by the alphabet.

Guide a discussion that helps children decide which type of reading they like better—stories or books and articles that give information.

We Read Together

Social Studies Link

31

Friends Help Friends

Social Studies Link

POLICE

21

ON MY WAY PRACTICE READER
Valentine Cat Sat, Sat, Sat

Valentine Cat
Sat, Sat, Sat
by Debora Silveira
illustrated by Clive Scruton

On My Way
Practice Reader

Houghton Mifflin

Preparing to Read

Building Background Have children tell about the cover illustration. Point out the cat's heart-shaped tag and explain that her name is *Valentine*. Read the title together. Then ask children what the animals do when they want to take a "cat nap."

Supporting the Reading

Preview the story to prepare children to read independently.

page 1: What did Valentine do first? Do you think she wants to take a cat nap?

page 2: What is new in this scene? What is the dog doing? Do you think Valentine likes to have the dog copy her? Why?

pages 4–6: Name the new animals. What are they doing? How does Valentine feel about that?

page 7: What is the girl doing? Can you find the word *call*? Follow along as I read what she calls to her cat. Now you read that with me. Do you know where the cat is?

Prompting Strategies

- Read that line again. Point to each word to be sure you say each one.
- What is the first sound in that word? Do you know the other sounds? Let's blend them.
- You said _____. Does that have the right sounds? Does it make sense?

Responding

Build Fluency Invite children to take turns reading aloud their favorite parts.

Extend Ask children to draw and write about what they think Valentine should do the next time she wants a cat nap.

Books for Small-Group Reading

The materials listed below provide reading practice for children at different levels.

Vocabulary Reader

How to Make a Salad

Leveled Reader

A Party

Little Big Books

Reading
My Dad and I
by Julia Ricardo Baerga
illustrated by Joe Cepeda

Aaron and Gayla's Alphabet Book
Pictures by Jan Spivey Gilchrist
Written by Eloise Greenfield
Reading
ABC

Little Readers for Guided Reading

LITTLE READERS
FOR GUIDED READING

Houghton Mifflin Classroom Bookshelf

OBJECTIVES

- Build and read words with consonants and short *a*.
- Make sentences with high-frequency words.

Materials

- **Letter Cards** *a, b, c, h, m, r, s, t, v*
- **Word Cards** *a, I, like, my, see, to*
- **Picture Cards** for sentence building
- **Punctuation Card** period

PHONICS
Consonants, Short *a* Words

❶ Review

Review building short *a* words. If some children need extra practice with the short *a* words, here is a menu of activities you can provide.

- Have children repeat the **Phonics Center** Activity for Day 4 with you in a small group.

- Provide tactile letters (letter tiles, sandpaper or foam letters) to have children make *cat, bat, hat, mat, rat, sat.*

- Reread the **Phonics Library** story "Cat Sat" with children. Focus specifically on short *a* words.

HIGH-FREQUENCY WORDS

a, I, like, my, see, to

❷ Review

Review the high-frequency words from the Word Wall.

- Give small groups the **Word Cards, Picture Cards,** and **Punctuation Cards** needed to make a sentence. Each child holds one card.

- Children stand and arrange themselves to make a sentence for others to read.

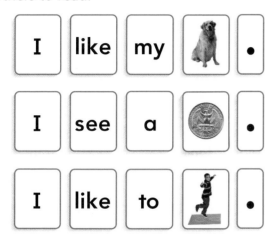

❸ Practice/Apply

- Children can complete **Practice Book** page 158 independently and read it to you during small group time.

- Pass out copies of the *I Like to* 📖, **Practice Book** pages 225–226. Read the title aloud. Ask children to tell who is speaking. Point to the boy and tell children that he is telling the story.

For each page, have children look at the picture and tell what the boy and his sisters are doing. Have them read the page silently. Then have a child read the page aloud. Use questions such as the following to prompt discussion:

Pages 1–3 What is the boy trying to do? What problem is he having? What do you think he should do?

Page 4 How did he solve his problem? What do you think of his idea?

Then have children count the high-frequency words in the story: How many times can you find the word *I* in this story? the word *see*? the word *like*? the word *to*? the word *my*? the word *a*?

Children can practice reading both high-frequency words and decodable words by rereading the **Phonics Library** story "Cat Sat."

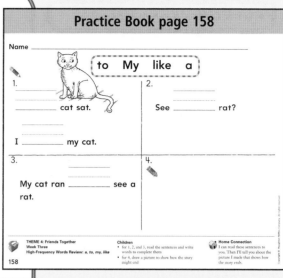

Practice Book page 158

Practice Book pages 225–226

Monitoring Student Progress

If . . .	Then . . .
children pause at high-frequency words while reading,	have partners practice reading the words on the Word Wall.

OBJECTIVES

- Blend consonants with short *a* to read words.

Materials

- Letter Cards *a, b, c, h, m, n, r, s, t, v*

BUILDING WORDS
Words with Short *a*

Model building the word *bat*.

- Display **Letter Cards** *a, b, c, h, m, n, r, s, t,* and *v*.

- How many sounds do you hear in *bat?* The first sound is /b/. I'll put up a *b* to spell that. What letter stands for the middle sound, /ă/? I'll add an *a* to spell that. The last sound is /t/. What letter stands for that sound? I'll add a *t* to spell that sound.

- Now I'm going to say a word. You write what I say. Listen: *mat.*

- Continue with *hat, vat, rat, cat,* and *sat.*

Check Understanding Ask children to write additional short *a* words such as *vat* on their white boards. Provide corrections as needed. Select individuals to read the words they've written.

Extend Practice Continue the activity with *ham, vat, van,* and *man.* Exaggerate the final sound in each word to help children name the correct final consonant. Then have children read the sentence *I see my cat,* blending the sounds for the last word. (Underlined words are from the Word Wall.)

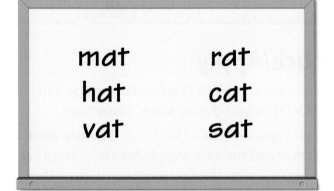

mat	rat
hat	cat
vat	sat

Challenge

As children become adept at reading short *a* words, they may suggest words like *chat, flat,* and *flap.* Help children sound out these words.

INDEPENDENT WRITING
Journals

OBJECTIVES
- Write independently.

Materials
- journals

Preparing to Write

- Journal writing should be a spontaneous writing activity. But sometimes children need an idea to spark their writing.

- For such times, make a list of topics that match a wide variety of interests in your classroom. When a writer is "stuck," suggest an idea from the list.

Writing Independently

- Remind writers that action words make their writing lively.

- Also point out that good writers write from left to right and use their best penmanship.

Portfolio Opportunity

Let children participate in the selection of journal entries to save and share with parents.

A Party

Summary: *This book describes all the special things that are associated with a birthday party. Readers see and read about a balloon, a hat, a present, a game, a toy, and a cake. It's a party!*

Story Words

This *p. 2*

is *p. 2*

High-Frequency Word

New Word

a *p. 2*

▲ ON LEVEL

Building Background and Vocabulary

Tell children that this book describes all the different things that are part of a birthday party. Preview the illustrations with children. Ask children to talk about why it's fun to celebrate birthdays. Encourage children to share their own ideas about the kinds of things they enjoy at a birthday party.

Comprehension Skill: Cause and Effect

Read together the Strategy Focus on the book flap. Remind children to use the strategy and, as they read, to think about why each pictured item plays a special part at a birthday party.

Responding

Discussing the Book Encourage children to talk about what they liked best about the story. Have children point to sentences or illustrations they enjoyed. Ask children to talk about which items have been part of their own birthday celebrations.

Responding Work with children to answer the questions on the inside back cover. Then help them complete the Writing and Drawing activity. Have children take turns sharing their drawings with classmates. Encourage them to explain why they enjoy that special party activity. Staple the pictures together to make a class book titled *Party Fun*.

▲ Student Book, Inside Back Cover

Responding

Think About What You Have Read

1. What is the story about?
   a birthday party
2. What things can you see at the party?
   a balloon, hat, gift, game, toy, cake

✎ **Writing and Drawing**

Draw a picture of something you like to do at a party.

LEVELED READERS

WEEK 3

Building Fluency

Model As children follow along in their books, reread pages 2 and 3. Point out that the first three words, *This is a*, on the two pages are the same. Explain to children that these words begin every page in the book.

Practice Have children work with partners. For each page, have one partner read the repeating phrase and the other child read the naming word that describes the picture. Have partners change roles and then reread the story. Encourage them to reread the book several times until each child can read all the pages aloud smoothly.

Oral Language Development

Naming Words Tell children that some words are naming words. Explain that naming words are words that name a thing, such as a *toy* or a *game*. Have children page through the story, pointing to the naming word on each page (*balloon, hat, present, game, toy, cake, party*). After they find each word on a page, have them look at the illustration and describe what they see. Encourage children to list other naming words that tell things they can see at a birthday party, such as *candle, ribbon,* or *ice cream*.

Practice Ask children to work with partners. Have each pair take turns pointing out classroom objects and telling the name for each object.

High-Frequency Word
New Word: *a*

Display the Word Card for *a*. Read the word aloud. Ask children to listen for the word as you read page 2 in *A Party*. Then have them turn to page 4 in the story. Point to the Word Card and ask children to point to the word *a* in the text. Then ask children to read the two sentences on pages 4 and 5 together.

a

Assessing Student Progress

Throughout Theme 4, you monitored student progress by using the following program features: the **Emerging Literacy Survey, Guiding Comprehension** questions, **skill lesson applications,** the **Theme 4 Observation Checklist,** and the **Monitoring Student Progress** boxes.

Your students are now ready for theme assessments, which allow you to assess each student's progress formally.

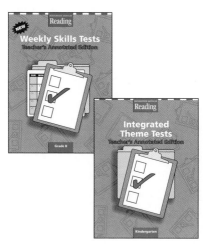

Testing Options and Multiple Measures

The **Integrated Theme Test** and the **Weekly Skills Tests** are formal group assessments used to evaluate children's performance on theme objectives. Administer the **Weekly Skills Test** at the end of each week. (**Theme Skills Tests** are also available for administration at the end of each theme, beginning with Theme 2.) The **Integrated Theme Test** for Themes 1–4 can be administered at the end of this theme, too.

In addition, other multiple measures might include: the **Emerging Literacy Survey** (either using previous results or administering again at the conclusion of the theme), the **Theme 4 Observation Checklist,** and **student writing** or **art-work** (both teacher- and student-selected). Multiple measures or assessment can be collected in a portfolio.

Fluency Assessment

Oral reading fluency is a useful measure of a child's development. In the early stages, oral fluency should be observed informally. You can use the **Leveled Reading Passages Assessment Kit** to assess fluency.

Technology

Managing Assessment

The **Learner Profile CD-ROM** lets you record, manage, and report the results of children's progress.

Using Assessment to Plan Instruction

Besides the results of theme assessments, you can use the **Theme 4 Observation Checklist** on the next page to determine individual children's needs and determine how to customize instruction of major kindergarten concepts for Theme 5.

Name _____ Date _____

Observation Checklist

	Beginning	Developing	Proficient
Listening Comprehension/ Oral Language/Vocabulary • Participates in story discussions			
• Listens to a story attentively			
Phonemic Awareness • Blends and segments onsets and rimes			
• Blends phonemes			
Phonics • Recognizes sounds for *h, c, v*			
• Blends and builds words with short *a*			
Concepts of Print • Recognizes spaces between words; first letter in a written word			
• Matches speech to print			
Reading and Fluency • Reads simple decodable texts			
Vocabulary: High-Frequency Words • Reads the high-frequency words *a, to*			
Comprehension • Recognizes organization; can summarize a familiar text			
• Understands cause and effect			
Writing and Language • Writes simple phrases or sentences			
• Participates in shared and interactive writing			

Copy this form for each child. Write notes or checkmarks in the appropriate columns.
The **Observation Checklist** also appears on **Blackline Master** 61.

Resources for Theme 4

Contents

Hattie Horse's Song
(TUNE: THE WHEELS ON THE BUS)

Use this music for Hattie Horse's song.

Hat- tie   is   a   hun- gry   horse.

She's   hun- gry   for   her   hay   of   course.

Hat- tie   is   a   hun- gry   horse.

She   hur- ries   home   at   noon.

NOTE: The measures of rest indicate instrumental interludes in the recorded music. If you are singing the song without the recording, these rest sections may be omitted.

Hattie Horse's Song

(tune: The Wheels on the Bus)

Hattie is a hungry horse.

She's hungry for her hay, of course.

Hattie is a hungry horse.

She hurries home at noon.

R2   **THEME 4: Friends Together**

Vinny Volcano's Song
(TUNE: ON TOP OF OLD SMOKEY)

Use this music for Vinny Volcano's song.

Vin-ny Vol- ca- no   is   my va- len-   tine.

Vin-ny Vol- ca- no,   oh   won't you be   mine?

I'll vi- sit Vin-   ny   in the   val-ley be-   low.

I'll bring some vio-   lets   and a   new vi- de-   o!

Vinny Volcano's Song
(tune: On Top of Old Smokey)
Vinny Volcano is my valentine.
Vinny Volcano, oh won't you be mine?
I'll visit Vinny in the valley below.
I'll bring some violets and a new video.

Music R3

Callie Cat's Song
(TUNE: YANKEE DOODLE)

Use this music for Callie Cat's song.

Cal- lie cat can   bake a   cake and   co- ver   it with   can- dy.

Cal- lie Cat can   bake some corn-bread.   Cal- lie   is so   han- dy.

Cal- lie bakes some cup-cakes, too. Her   cup- cakes are   so   ca- key.

Cal- lie bakes some coo- kies, too. Her   coo- kies are   so   fla- key.

Callie Cat's Song
(tune: Yankee Doodle)

Callie Cat can bake a cake and cover it with candy.

Callie Cat can bake some cornbread. Callie is so handy.

Callie bakes some cupcakes, too. Her cupcakes are so cakey.

Callie bakes some cookies, too. Her cookies are so flakey.

THEME RESOURCES

MUSIC

Andy Apple's Song
(TUNE: SKIP TO MY LOU)

Use this music for Andy Apple's song.

An- dy Ap-ple is an a- cro- bat. An-dy can jump way

ov-er his mat. Ant can catch him, just like that!

An- dy Ap- ple is an a- cro- bat.

NOTE: *The measures of rest indicate instrumental interludes in the recorded music. If you are singing the song without the recording, these rest sections may be omitted.*

Andy Apple's Song
(tune: Skip to My Lou)
Andy Apple is an acrobat.
Andy can jump way over his mat.
Ant can catch him, just like that!
Andy Apple is an acrobat.

WORD LIST

In Themes 1 through 3, the Phonics Library stories are wordless stories to develop oral language. Remaining themes feature the phonics skills and high-frequency words listed here.

THEME 1

Phonics Skills:
none taught in this theme
High-Frequency Words:
none taught in this theme

Phonics Library, Week 1:

We Go to School

wordless story

Phonics Library, Week 2:

See What We Can Do

wordless story

Phonics Library, Week 3:

We Can Make It

wordless story

THEME 2

Phonics Skills:
Initial consonants *s, m, r*
High-Frequency Words: *I, see*

Phonics Library, Week 1:

My Red Boat

wordless story

Phonics Library, Week 2:

Look at Me!

wordless story

Phonics Library, Week 3:

The Parade

wordless story

THEME 3

Phonics Skills:
Initial consonants *t, b, n*
High-Frequency Words: *my, like*

Phonics Library, Week 1:

The Birthday Party

wordless story

Phonics Library, Week 2:

Baby Bear's Family

wordless story

Phonics Library, Week 3:

Cat's Surprise

wordless story

THEME 4

Phonics Skills:
Initial consonants *h, v, c;* words with short *a*
High-Frequency Words: *a, to*

Phonics Library, Week 1:

Nat at Bat

Words with short *a*: at, bat, hat, Nat, sat
High-Frequency Words: *my, see*

Phonics Library, Week 2:

A Vat

Words with short *a*: hat, mat, rat, vat
High-Frequency Word: *a*

Phonics Library, Week 3:

Cat Sat

Words with short *a*: bat, cat, hat, mat, sat
High-Frequency Words: *my, see*

THEME 5

Phonics Skills:
Initial consonants *p, g, f;* words with short *a*
High-Frequency Words: *and, go*

Phonics Library, Week 1:

Nat, Pat, and Nan

Words with short *a*: Nan, ran, Nat, Pat, sat
High-Frequency Words: *and, see*

Phonics Library, Week 2:

Go, Cat!

Words with short *a*: Nan, ran, Van, Cat, Pat, sat
High-Frequency Word: *go*

Phonics Library, Week 3:

Pat and Nan

Words with short *a*: fan, Nan, ran, Pat, sat
High-Frequency Words: *a, and, go*

THEME 6

Phonics Skills:
Initial consonants *l, k, q;* words with short *i*
High-Frequency Words: *is, here*

Phonics Library, Week 1:

Can It Fit?

Words with short *i*: fit, it, sit
Words with short *a*: can, man, van
High-Frequency Words: *a, go, I, is, my*

Phonics Library, Week 2:

Kit

Words with short *i*: bit, fit, it, Kit, lit, sit
Words with short *a*: can, pan, hat
High-Frequency Words: *a, here, I*

Phonics Library, Week 3:

Fan

Words with short *i*: bit, quit
Words with short *a*: an, Fan, sat
High-Frequency Words: *a, here, is*

THEME 7

Phonics Skills:
Initial consonants *d, z;* words with short *i*
High-Frequency Words: *for, have*

Phonics Library, Week 1:

Big Rig

Words with short *i*: Big, dig, Rig, pit
Words with short *a*: can, Dan
High-Frequency Words: *a, for*

Phonics Library, Week 2:

Tan Van

Words with short *i*: *Pig, Zig, it*

Words with short *a*: *can, Dan, ran, tan, van, Cat, sat*

High-Frequency Words: *a, have, I, is*

Phonics Library, Week 3:

Zig Pig and Dan Cat

Words with short *i*: *dig, Pig, Zig, it*

Words with short *a*: *can, Dan, Cat, sat*

High-Frequency Words: *and, for, have, here, I, is*

THEME 8

Phonics Skills:
Consonant *x*; words with short *o*

High-Frequency Words: *said, the*

Phonics Library, Week 1:

Dot Got a Big Pot

Words with short *o*: *Dot, got, hot, lot, pot*

Words with short *i*: *big, it*

Words with short *a*: *Nan, Nat, sat*

High-Frequency Words: *a, and, I, is, like, said*

Phonics Library, Week 2:

The Big, Big Box

Words with short *o*: *box, Fox, not*

Words with short *i*: *big, bit, fit, hit, it*

Words with short *a*: *can, Dan, Fan, Cat, hat, mat, sat*

High-Frequency Words: *a, is, my, said, the*

Phonics Library, Week 3:

A Pot for Dan Cat

Words with short *o*: *pot, Fox*

Words with short *i*: *big, fit*

Words with short *a*: *can, Dan, Fan, ran, Cat, sat*

High-Frequency Words: *a, and, for, I, see, said*

THEME 9

Phonics Skills:
Initial consonants *w, y*; words with short *e*

High-Frequency Words: *play, she*

Phonics Library, Week 1:

Get Set! Play!

Words with short *e*: *get, set, wet*

Words with short *o*: *got, not, Fox*

Words with short *i*: *Pig*

Words with short *a*: *can*

High-Frequency Words: *a, I, play, said*

Phonics Library, Week 2:

Ben

Words with short *e*: *Ben, Hen, men, ten, get, net, pet, vet, yet*

Words with short *o*: *got, not, box, Fox*

Words with short *i*: *it*

Words with short *a*: *can*

High-Frequency Words: *a, I, my, play, said, the*

Phonics Library, Week 3:

Pig Can Get Wet

Words with short *e*: *get, wet*

Words with short *o*: *got, not*

Words with short *i*: *big, Pig, wig, sit*

Words with short *a*: *can, Cat, sat*

High-Frequency Words: *a, my, play, said, she*

THEME 10

Phonics Skills:
Initial consonant *j*; words with short *u*

High-Frequency Words: *are, he*

Phonics Library, Week 1:

Ken and Jen

Words with short *u*: *dug*

Words with short *e*: *Ken, Jen, wet*

Words with short *o*: *hot*

Words with short *i*: *big, dig, it, pit*

High-Frequency Words: *a, and, are, is*

Phonics Library, Week 2:

It Can Fit

Words with short *u*: *but, nut, jug, lug, rug*

Words with short *o*: *box, not*

Words with short *i*: *big, fit, it*

Words with short *a*: *can, tan, van, fat, hat*

High-Frequency Words: *a, he, see, she*

Phonics Library, Week 3:

The Bug Hut

Words with short *u*: *but, Bug, hug, lug, hut*

Words with short *o*: *box, Dot, got, not*

Words with short *i*: *Big, jig*

Words with short *a*: *can, Jan, fat, hat*

High-Frequency Words: *a, here, is, she, the*

Cumulative Word List

By the end of Theme 10, children will have been taught the skills necessary to read the following words.

Words with short a

at, bat, cat, fat, hat, mat, Nat, Pat, rat, sat, vat, an, ban, can, Dan, fan, Jan, man, Nan, pan, ran, tan, van

Words with short i

bit, fit, hit, it, kit, lit, pit, quit, sit, wit, big, dig, fig, jig, pig, rig, wig, zig

Words with short o

cot, dot, got, hot, jot, lot, not, pot, rot, tot, box, fox, ox

Words with short e

bet, get, jet, let, met, net, pet, set, vet, wet, yet, Ben, den, hen, Jen, Ken, men, pen, ten

Words with short u

bug, dug, hug, jug, lug, mug, rug, tug, but, cut, hut, jut, nut, rut

High-Frequency Words

a, and, are, for, go, have, he, here, I, is, like, my, play, said, see, she, the, to

I

See

see

My

my

Like

like

Use for Theme 4, Word Wall.

A

To

a

to

Use for Theme 4, Word Wall.

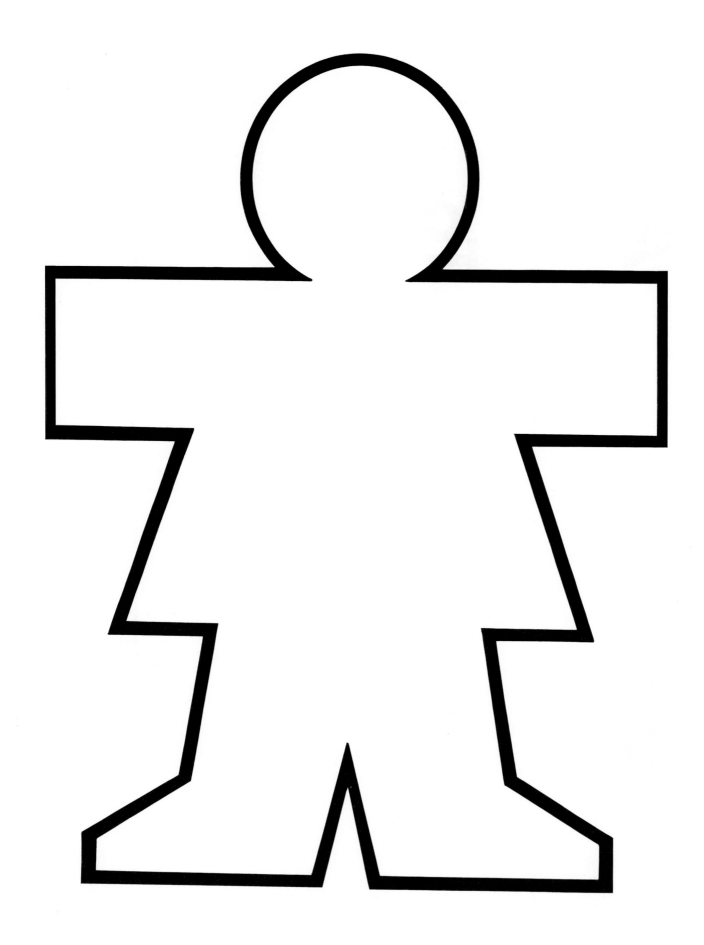

Shape Paper for The Writing Center   Use for Theme 4.

My Journal

Name _____

My Reading Log

I can read

My new words

_____   _____

- - - - - - - - - - - - - -   - - - - - - - - - - - - - -

_____   _____

Name: _____

I can count to ___!

Date: _____

Use for Theme 4, Wrap-Up.

TECHNOLOGY RESOURCES

American Melody
P. O. Box 270
Guilford, CT 06437
800-220-5557
www.americanmelody.com

Audio Bookshelf
174 Prescott Hill Road
Northport, ME 04849
800-234-1713
www.audiobookshelf.com

Baker & Taylor
100 Business Center Drive
Pittsburgh, PA 15205
800-775-2600
www.btal.com

BDD Audio/Random House
400 Hohn Road
Westminster, MD 21157
800-733-3000

Big Kids Productions
1606 Dywer Avenue
Austin, TX 78704
800-477-7811
www.bigkidsvideo.com

Books on Tape
P.O. Box 25122
Santa Ana, CA 92799
www.booksontape.com
800-541-5525

Broderbund Company
1 Martha's Way
Hiawatha, IA 52233
800-716-8506
www.broderbund.com

Filmic Archives
The Cinema Center
Botsford, CT 06404
800-366-1920
www.filmicarchives.com

Great White Dog Picture Company
10 Toon Lane
Lee, NH 03824
800-397-7641
www.greatwhitedog.com

HarperAudio
10 E. 53rd Street
New York, NY 10022
800-242-7737
www.harperaudio.com

Houghton Mifflin Company
222 Berkeley Street
Boston, MA 02116
800-225-3362

Informed Democracy
P.O. Box 67
Santa Cruz, CA 95063
800-827-0949

JEF Films
143 Hickory Hill Circle
Osterville, MA 02655
508-428-7198

Kimbo Educational
P. O. Box 477
Long Branch, NJ 07740
800-631-2187
www.kimboed.com

Library Video Co.
P. O. Box 580
Wynnewood, PA 19096
800-843-3620
wwww.libraryvideo.com

Listening Library
P.O. Box 25122
Santa Ana, CA 92799
800-541-5525
www.listeninglibrary.com

Live Oak Media
P. O. Box 652
Pine Plains, NY 12567
800-788-1121
www.liveoakmedia.com

Media Basics
Lighthouse Square
P.O. Box 449
Guilford, CT 06437
800-542-2505
www.mediabasicsvideo.com

Microsoft Corp.
One Microsoft Way
Redmond, WA 98052
800-426-9400
www.microsoft.com

National Geographic School Publishing
P.O. Box 10597
Des Moines, IA 50340
800-368-2728
www.nationalgeographic.com

New Kid Home Video
P.O. Box 10443
Beverly Hills, CA 90213
800-309-2392
www.NewKidhomevideo.com

Puffin Books
345 Hudson Street
New York, NY 10014
800-233-7364

Rainbow Educational Media
4540 Preslyn Drive
Raleigh, NC 27616
800-331-4047
www.rainbowedumedia.com

Recorded Books
270 Skipjack Road
Prince Frederick, MD 20678
800-638-1304
www.recordedbooks.com

Sony Wonder
Dist. by Professional Media Service
19122 S. Vermont Avenue
Gardena, CA 90248
800-223-7672
www.sonywonder.com

Spoken Arts
195 South White Rock Road
Holmes, NY 12531
800-326-4090
www.spokenartsmedia.com

SRA Media
220 E. Danieldale Road
DeSoto, TX 75115
800-843-8855
www.sra4kids.com

Sunburst Technology
1550 Executive Drive
Elgin, IL, 60123
800-321-7511
www.sunburst.com

SVE & Churchill Media
6677 North Northwest Highway
Chicago, IL 60631
800-829-1900
www.svemedia.com

Tom Snyder Productions
80 Coolidge Hill Road
Watertown, MA 02472
800-342-0236
www.tomsnyder.com

Troll Communications
100 Corporate Drive
Mahwah, NJ 07430
800-526-5289
www.troll.com

Weston Woods
143 Main Street
Norwalk, CT 06851-1318
800-243-5020
www.scholastic.com/westonwoods

Index

Boldface page references indicate formal strategy and skill instruction.

A

Acquiring English, students. *See* English Language Learners.

Activating prior knowledge. *See* Background, building.

Alphabetic principle
  letter and sound match, T36, T60, T94, T108, T118, T152, T162, T172
  letter names, T28, T36, T86, T94, T144, T152
  recognizing letters, T28, T36, T86, T94, T144, T152

Areas. *See* Centers.

Assessment
  Formal Assessment. *See* Theme Assessment Wrap-Up, T184–T185
  Informal Assessment. *See* Observation Checklist.
  Monitoring Student Progress, T39, T49, T50, T61, T69, T97, T106, T108, T119, T127, T155, T161, T162, T173, T181
  Planning for, T12–T13
  Portfolio Opportunity, T71, T106, T129, T161, T183

B

Background, building
  concept development, T26, T34, T58, T82, T92, T116, T140, T170, T179
  prior knowledge, T34, T92, T140, T150, T160, T170
  See also English Language Learners.

Bibliography, T4–T5

Big Book selections
  ABC book
    From Apples to Zebras: A Book of ABC's, T60, T118, T172
  fiction
    Aaron and Gayla's Alphabet Book by Eloise Greenfield, T33, T43-T49, T66, T149, T178
    My Dad and I by Julio Ricardo Baerga, T91, T99, T101, T124, T159, T178
  nonfiction
    Friends Help Friends, T66, T115, T124, T177, T178
    We Read Together, T57, T66, T169, T178

rhymes
    Higglety Pigglety: A Book of Rhymes, **T25,** T30, **T33,** T39, **T57, T65,** T88, T97, T101, T139, T146, **T159, T169**

Blending, T50, T51, T52, T53, T54, T60–T61, T62, T70, T108, T109, T110, T111, T112, T118–119, T120, T128, T162, T163, T163, T164, T165, T166, T172–T173, T174, T182

Book awareness. *See* Concepts of print.

Books for Small-Group Reading
  Houghton Mifflin Classroom Bookshelf, T67, T125, T179
  Little Big Books, T67, T125, T179
  Little Readers for Guided Reading, T67, T125, T179
  On My Way Practice Reader, T179
  Phonics Library: Decodable Text. *See* Phonics Library.
  Word and Picture Books, T39, T97, T155

Brainstorming, T167

C

Cause-effect relationships. *See* Comprehension skills.

CD-ROMs, T28, T86, T162

Centers
  art, T33, T35, T41, T91, T93, T99, T139, T149, T151, T157
  book, T25, T27, T83
  phonics, **T29, T37, T61, T87, T95, T119, T145, T153, T173**
  writing, T31, T49, T63, T81, T89, T107, T121, T141, T147, T161, T175

Challenge. *See* Reaching All Learners.

Classroom management
  independent groups, T27, T29, T37, T39, T49, T50, T51–T53, T61, T67, T69, T83, T87, T95, T97, T106, T108, T109–T111, T119, T125, T127, T141, T145, T153, T155, T162, T163–T165, T173, T181
  individuals, T33, T50, T54, T60, T66, T69, T108, T118, T124, T127, T145, T155, T157, T162, T172, T173, T174, T178, T182
  partners, T39, T61, T66, T67, T69, T120, T125, T157, T174, T181

teacher-led groups, T27, T29, T37, T39, T49, T50, T51–T53, T61, T67, T69, T83, T87, T95, T97, T106, T108, T109–T111, T125, T127, T141, T145, T153, T155, T162, T163–T165, T173, T181
whole class, T24–T25, T26–T27, T28–T29, T32–T33, T34–T35, T36–T37, T38–T39, T42–T43, T44–T49, T50, T56–T57, T60–T61, T64–T65, T66–T67, T68–T69, T80–T81, T82–T85, T86–T87, T90–T91, T92–T93, T94–T95, T96–T97, T100–T101, T102–T107, T108, T114–T115, T118–T119, T122–T123, T124–T125, T126–T127, T138–T139, T140–T143, T144–T145, T148–T149, T150–T153, T154–T155, T158–T159, T160–T161, T162, T168–T169, T170, T171, T172–T173, T176–T177, T178, T179, T180–T181

Combination Classroom, T14

Compare/contrast. *See* Comprehension skills.

Comprehension skills
  cause and effect, **T124, T48, T82, T92, T103, T116, T140, T160, T171**
  conclusions, drawing, **T103, T104**
  details, noting, **T46, T59, T103, T104**
  judgments, making, **T116, T171**
  predicting outcomes, **T59**
  sequence of events, **T47**
  text organization and summarizing, **T26, T34, T45, T45, T48, T58, T66, T150, T151, T170, T178**

Comprehension strategies. *See* Strategies, reading.

Concepts of print
  beginning/end of written word, **T59**
  match spoken word to print, **T105, T30, T88, T146, T117**
  one-to-one word match, **T30, T88, T146**
  word spacing, **T45, T104, T150, T170**
  See also Mechanics, language.

Content areas, reading in the. *See* Cross-curricular links.

Cooperative learning activities, T27, T29, T37, T39, T40, T50, T55, T61, T62, T63, T66, T67, T68, T69, T70, T83, T87, T95, T97, T98, T106, T108, T112, T113, T119, T120, T121, T124, T125, T127, T128, T141, T145, T153, T155, T157, T162, T167, T173, T174, T175, T178, T180, T181